He saw early that trust is not a slogan; it is an operating system. *The Answer Economy* is essential reading."

**—Norm Johnston**

*SVP, Head of Global Advertising Strategy, News Corp; Former Global CEO, Unruly; Author,* Adaptive Marketing

"We've spent decades optimizing brands for search engines, social platforms, and digital experiences. Now we must optimize for AI-mediated discovery and decision-making. Pete Blackshaw offers marketers an insightful and timely framework for succeeding in this new reality, where trust, evidence, and authoritative content increasingly determine who gets recommended. *The Answer Economy* is thought-provoking, highly actionable, and belongs on every executive's desk."

**—Michael Donnelly**

*EVP - AI, MarTech, and Marketing Futures, Association of National Advertisers (ANA)*

"Pete Blackshaw's *The Answer Economy* takes the core Zero Moment of Truth insight into the LLM era, where AI-generated answers increasingly shape what consumers see, trust, and choose. It is a clear, practical handbook for all marketers who need to understand this new reality and act on it."

**—Jim Lecinski**

*Author,* Winning the Zero Moment of Truth (ZMOT) *and* The AI Marketing Canvas*; Clinical Professor of Marketing, Kellogg School of Management, Northwestern University*

"This pathfinding book nails the uncomfortable truth most organizations avoid—AI isn't asking better questions, it's exposing that brands just aren't explaining what consumers want to know. AI has become judge and jury on brand merits. The only way to close that gap is with structured, objective data."

**—Jeff Goldstein**

*COO, ACUPOLL Precision Research*

"Unlike past digital disruptions, GenAI is being driven top-down—from the C-suite outward. *The Answer Economy* gives marketers, technologists, and operators the clear, grounded frameworks they need to win the prompted moment of truth and deliver on executive expectations."

**—Rich Guest**

*Global EVP Marketing; Cannes Lions Winner; former IMAX, Burger King, DDB; Faculty, USC Annenberg*

"I've known Pete since our days at P&G and later helped build PlanetFeedback with him. For decades, he's consistently identified the shifts that matter before they become obvious. In *The Answer Economy*, he does it again—spotlighting the AI-driven trust revolution every CMO and brand builder now needs to understand."

**—Mike Nazzaro**
*CEO, Claritas; Former P&G; Co-Builder, PlanetFeedback*

"This book will help you not just as a marketer or technologist—but as a person. Pete Blackshaw reframes trust and honesty during the most consequential pivot in our industry in a quarter century. Trust is built through small, repeatable, honest, consistent actions every day. In *The Answer Economy*, you'll learn how those actions—for brands and organizations of every size—are defined by their consistency at the prompted moment of truth."

**—Al Reid**
*President, Saatchi & Saatchi West*

"Pete goes beyond the current exuberance of AI to provide specific actions your brand can take to survive and thrive in a world of LLMs owning your company narrative. A thoughtful primer on how organizations must adapt to both ephemeral customer behavior and ever-evolving technology—or be left behind."

**—David Dintenfass**
*President, Enterprise Growth, Humana;*
*Former Chief Marketing Officer, Fidelity Investments*

"Marketers once crafted messages for consumers. Now they must build credibility for machines. The intermediary has changed. The stakes have never been higher. And Blackshaw delivers exactly the insights marketers today so urgently need."

**—Jeffrey Rayport**
*Faculty, Entrepreneurial Management Unit,*
*Harvard Business School*

"In *The Answer Economy*, brands are not just built in the marketplace—they are built in the answers consumers trust. Pete Blackshaw shows leaders how to rethink brand building, innovation, and trust for an AI-mediated world."

**—Leigh Radford**
*Corporate Board Member; Retired Senior Vice President,*
*Procter & Gamble; Founder, P&G Ventures*

"*The Answer Economy* captures a shift every modern brand and technology leader needs to understand: in an AI-mediated world, R&D is the new marketing. Pete Blackshaw shows why scientific evidence, substantiated claims, and trusted consistent content are becoming the infrastructure that determines how brands are discovered, evaluated, and chosen."

**—Tiffani Sossei**
*SVP, Head of Commercial & R&D Technology, Kenvue*

"If you care about your brand's future, this is a book to keep close. Pete Blackshaw lays out a practical, chapter-by-chapter guide to navigating an AI-driven marketplace. A smart, timely read for any leader trying to stay ahead of what's coming next."

**—Tara Marotti**
*CEO, Burke, Inc.*

"In healthcare, trust is everything—and who gets to answer the billions of questions people are asking about their health is now up for grabs. *The Answer Economy* gives leaders the framework and road map to compete in the AI-driven search era. Every search is a plea for clarity and reassurance. This book shows who earns the answer."

**—Todd Unger**
*Chief Experience Officer, American Medical Association (AMA)*

"Every marketer now serves two audiences: one human, one machine. The human is emotional, sensitive, and gloriously lazy. The machine is unemotional, insensitive, loves facts, and never tires. You cannot win both with one playbook. *The Answer Economy* is the first book to take that seriously, giving leaders and marketers the metrics to see clearly, the behaviors that build trust at scale, and a 100-day plan to act. This isn't a marketing book; it's an operating manual for a market that has already changed."

**—Veronika Kryuchkova**
*Global Head of Capability Building, Marketing Academy, Reckitt*

HOW AI AGENTS WILL
DECIDE YOUR BRAND'S FUTURE

# THE ANSWER ECONOMY

PETE BLACKSHAW

WILEY

Published by John Wiley & Sons, Inc., Hoboken, New Jersey.



For general information on our other products and services or for technical support, please contact our Customer Care Department within the United States at (800) 762-2974, outside the United States at (317) 572-3993 or fax (317) 572-4002.

Wiley also publishes its books in a variety of electronic formats. Some content that appears in print may not be available in electronic formats. For more information about Wiley products, visit our website at www.wiley.com.

***Library of Congress Cataloging-in-Publication Data:***

Names: Blackshaw, Pete author | John Wiley & Sons publisher
Title: The answer economy : how AI agents will decide your brand's future / Pete Blackshaw.
Description: Hoboken, New Jersey : Wiley, [2026] | Includes index.
Identifiers: LCCN 2026024173 (print) | LCCN 2026024174 (ebook) | ISBN 9781394432592 cloth | ISBN 9781394432615 adobe pdf | ISBN 9781394432608 epub
Subjects: LCSH: Intelligent agents (Computer software)—Business applications | Artificial intelligence—Business applications | Advertising—Technological innovations
Classification: LCC HF5548.2 .B523 2026 (print) | LCC HF5548.2 (ebook)
LC record available at https://lccn.loc.gov/2026024173
LC ebook record available at https://lccn.loc.gov/2026024174

Cover Design: Wiley
Cover Image: Bakhtiar Zein/Shutterstock
Author Photo: Courtesy of Philip Heidenreich
Printed and bound by CPI Group (UK) Ltd, Croydon, CR0 4YY

C9781394432592_030826

*For my children,* **Liam***,* **Leila***, and* **Sophia***—*
*the Answer Generation.*

*You are growing up in a world full of unanswered questions—*
*about what work matters, what skills endure,*
*and how trust is earned.*

**Keep asking the right questions.**
**Don't settle for easy answers.**

—

**For John Pepper**

*For your friendship and mentorship,*
*and for showing that true leadership*
*is not about having the answers,*
*but about asking the right questions—*
*with integrity, humility,*
*and an unwavering focus on the consumer.*

# Contents

# A Note on How This Book Was Made

That this book about AI accountability drew on AI assistance along the way isn't irony—it's proof of concept.

**Claude** served as my primary collaboration partner: structuring arguments, stress-testing frameworks, and flagging unsubstantiated claims with the same bluntness I argue every brand should expect from answer engines. **ChatGPT** helped sharpen language, explore alternative framings, and generated all the illustrations. **Grok** provided useful provocation when I needed my assumptions challenged. **Google Gemini** was invaluable for sourcing and fact verification.

The Takeaway Tracks—the songs closing each chapter—are genuine collaborations: AI synthesized the chapter ideas into lyrical form; I pushed, reshaped, and rebuilt until they felt right. I then used my favorite AI song generator, **Suno**, to turn the lyrics into fully produced songs.

What AI didn't provide: the frameworks, the case studies, the career-long observations, or the voice. Every word in this book is mine. The AI helped me say it better.

I'd be remiss not to acknowledge my human editor **Angela Morrison**, who outperformed every AI in the stack. Her relentless focus on the foundations of great writing—particularly her crusade against indefinite pronouns—had me reaching for Strunk & White more times than I care to admit. No algorithm has yet replicated her gift for making you feel simultaneously grateful and humbled.

—*Pete Blackshaw*

# Introduction: The Bell Is Ringing Again

This book is not about artificial intelligence alone. This book is about what happens to brands when Artificial Intelligence (AI) systems begin answering questions—and shaping decisions—on behalf of consumers.

The Answer Economy describes a world where answers become the primary interface between brands and the people they serve. It rewards truth, usefulness, and consistency; it rewards brands that show up when questions are asked, not just when ads are served.

AI didn't create the shift toward questions and answers. It made that shift unavoidable.

In 2018, I gave a TEDx talk at the University of St. Gallen in Switzerland titled "The Concierge Economy," where I began exploring how brands would need to evolve from traditional marketing to service, and I posed a simple question: *Is your bell ringing?*

The idea was simple. In a world where consumers expect help, not just messaging, the "bell" is the signal—a moment when a customer raises their hand, asks a question, or needs guidance. The brands that win are the ones that hear it—and respond.

At the time, that bell rang intermittently. Today, it rings constantly. And we're just in the first inning of the AI revolution.

For more than a century, branding has been built on the art of persuasion—shaping perception through repetition, reach, and emotional appeal. That model worked because brands controlled the message, the media, and the moment. When attention was scarce and information traveled slowly, interruption wasn't a flaw; it was the strategy. The more memorable the interruption, the more powerful the brand.

Even at its peak, however, that system depended on a quiet assumption: that consumers would accept what they were told, or at least not push back too hard. Questions existed, but they were managed—filtered through focus groups, surveys, call centers, and carefully scripted FAQs. The public face of the brand remained largely one-way.

What AI changed wasn't curiosity. People have always had questions. What changed was the friction required to get answers—time, effort, and uncertainty.

AI collapsed that friction. It made asking instantaneous, private, and persistent. Instead of navigating menus or decoding marketing language, people could ask a question and receive an answer that felt direct, patient, and on their side.

Early analysis of large-scale AI interactions suggests that a significant portion of consumer AI usage now involves iterative collaboration—users refining prompts, validating outputs, and progressively delegating decision-making authority rather than simple automation. People aren't just asking questions anymore—they're starting to Ask Through (I'll unpack that idea in the chapters ahead).

This pattern reflects what I call the Answer Economy's defining characteristic: Economic value flows not to whoever provides information fastest, but to whoever is believed at the moment a decision is made.

## A House of Jingles

I grew up in a house of jingles. My father was a classic Madison Avenue archetype—an advertising executive at a fast-growing independent agency in Los Angeles during the industry's golden age. Our dinner table doubled as an open-plan creative department. We celebrated when a new campaign hit the air. I tagged along on commercial shoots around Southern California. I can still hum the jingles from Pacific Southwest Airlines and Great Western Savings without thinking.

The brands that surrounded me—Chevrolet, Pennzoil, Kahlúa, Suzuki, Neutrogena, Alpha Beta Super Markets, Vail—weren't just logos. They were cultural fixtures, repeated until they became familiar, trusted, almost comforting.

I absorbed the language of persuasion before I could drive: positioning statements, reach curves, frequency, share of voice. The logic was elegant and powerful. Say the right thing, to the right people, enough times, and the market would reward you.

And for a long time, it did.

Advertising was a one-way street. Brands talked. Consumers listened. The craft was in making interruption feel welcome—entertaining, emotional, memorable. It was a system that shaped industries, careers, and culture itself.

At the time, nothing about it felt broken.

## The Banana Slug: How Brands Actually Work

By the time I arrived at the University of California at Santa Cruz, I had absorbed more about branding than I realized—not from textbooks, but from proximity. Watching how my father's work took shape. How ideas moved from briefing rooms to storyboards to culture. I understood intuitively that brands weren't just names or logos. They were agreements—shortcuts for shared meaning.

At the University of California, Santa Cruz, I had an unexpected chance to put that understanding to work.

I attended Cowell College, part of the university's original residential college system, modeled loosely on Oxford and Cambridge. The idea wasn't just to educate students, but to immerse them in inquiry: small communities, big questions, debate as a way of learning.

When I arrived, the campus was in the middle of an intense student controversy.

For years, students had embraced the banana slug as the university's unofficial mascot. It was quirky, self-effacing, and deeply local—a creature that shared a symbiotic relationship with the California redwoods surrounding the campus. To students, the slug captured something essential about Santa Cruz: humility over bravado, ecology over ego, curiosity over aggression.

The administration saw it differently.

They worried the slug lacked seriousness. They squirmed at the idea of being represented by something so untraditional. At one point, they even blocked a student vote that would have made the banana slug official.

What was playing out wasn't about a mascot. It was about authority, identity, and who gets to define meaning.

I joined forces with my friend Marc Ratner to help give shape to what students already felt. Drawing on the branding instincts I'd grown up around, we set out to pour meaning into the nascent symbol—not through protest, but through interpretation.

We created an intellectual, semi-parodic character: a banana slug wearing round glasses and reading Plato. We took the University of California motto *Fiat Lux* ("Let there be light") and twisted it into *Fiat Slug* ("Let there be slug").

It started as satire—but satire wrapped in a mission.

The goal wasn't to mock the university, but to express its values in a way that felt authentic: thoughtful, self-aware, slightly irreverent, and open to participation. We printed T-shirts, mugs—anything we could screen-print.

Over time, the brand we helped shape made it easier for everyone—including a once-resistant administration—to embrace the slug. By the time I left Santa Cruz, the banana slug had become the university's official mascot. Years later, *Sports Illustrated* would dub it the nation's best college nickname.

And a few years after that, Quentin Tarantino put our design on John Travolta in *Pulp Fiction*—an unexpected cultural afterlife that elevated a once-dismissed campus symbol into something far larger than we could have imagined. At the time, I thought I was selling T-shirts. Only later did I fully appreciate what had happened.

A brand hadn't been declared. It had been negotiated. Meaning didn't come from authority. It came from participation.

I'm convinced the slug story tipped my application over the edge when I applied to Harvard Business School. I can almost hear the admissions committee now: If he can sell the banana slug, he can probably sell the Brooklyn Bridge.

## When the System Started to Break

Landing at Procter & Gamble after business school felt like a coronation. P&G wasn't just a company; it was the operating system behind modern brand building. If advertising was the art, P&G was the architecture. Everything had a framework. We didn't guess; we tested. We didn't improvise; we optimized. Share of shelf, share of voice, share of mind. Copy rotation. Concept testing. Media mix modeling. The discipline was intoxicating.

I felt like I had been admitted to a priesthood.

And then the internet arrived—inside the system. Not as a theory. Not as a sideshow. As something real, fast, and quietly destabilizing.

At first, we treated it as an efficiency upgrade. A faster channel. A better way to distribute the same messages. Banner ads instead of print. Email instead of direct mail. A new surface, same logic.

But the tools themselves kept whispering something else.

Consumers weren't just receiving messages anymore. They were clicking. Searching. Comparing. Asking. Sending emails. Posting comments. Doing things our models weren't designed to absorb.

We began experimenting with what we called *Interactive Marketing*. Not clickable banners, but actual interaction. Tools built around consumer questions.

The Tide Stain Detective. The Always Protection Selector. The Pampers Parenting Institute—these weren't ads. They were services.

And something unexpected happened.

The moment we stopped broadcasting and started responding, the energy changed. The relationship changed. The trust changed.

People weren't just engaging; they were inquiring. They weren't browsing; they were asking for help.

The discomfort set in at that moment.

If consumers were asking real questions—about safety, suitability, performance—why were we still treating answers as marketing collateral? Why were the most human moments being routed back into a system designed for persuasion, not help?

I didn't have language for it yet. I just knew the old playbook—clever message, massive reach, controlled narrative—was suddenly insufficient.

The model wasn't wrong. It was incomplete. It was the first signal that answering—not persuading—might become the real work of brand management.

## When Consumers Took the Microphone

The realization that the old playbook was insufficient followed me—consciously this time—when I left P&G in 1999 to start PlanetFeedback.

PlanetFeedback was one of the first platforms where consumers could publicly send compliments, complaints, and questions directly to brands—and have those interactions visible to others.

In hindsight, it was an early answer engine.

We aggregated thousands of individual stories. We made them searchable. We forced brands to respond in the open. Customer service stopped being a private cost center and became a form of public accountability.

Patterns emerged quickly. One mishandled interaction could become a symbol for something much larger. Trust didn't erode quietly; it collapsed publicly.

I became obsessed enough to write a book about it: *Satisfied Customers Tell Three Friends, Angry Customers Tell 3,000.* The title captured the leverage we were seeing: When everyone has a microphone, the cost of breaking trust multiplies.

What PlanetFeedback made unavoidable was this: Consumers weren't just venting. They were asking collective questions: Can I trust this company? Does this product do what it says? Will they treat me fairly when something goes wrong?

The answers didn't come from slogans. They emerged from patterns of real experience.

## The Cruelty of Permanent Memory

PlanetFeedback soon became part of Nielsen, where I continued working with the world's top brands on feedback, social media analysis, and word-of-mouth marketing.

But then I did something unexpected: I jumped back into the corporate scene.

Nestlé asked me to lead global digital and social media in their Swiss headquarters. I said yes—and walked straight into a firestorm.

Palm oil sourcing. Deforestation. Infant nutrition. Water extraction. Activists, journalists, and NGOs were relentless. Old controversies resurfaced alongside new ones.

We had a saying that came up in every late-night crisis meeting: *Google and Wikipedia never forget.* No matter how carefully crafted our sustainability reports were, one search could pull people back to decades-old grievances. Some fair. Some distorted. All sticky.

The lesson was brutal but clarifying: Operations and marketing had fused. What you did in your supply chain wasn't backstage anymore. Transparency wasn't optional. Truth had a half-life far longer than any campaign calendar.

I kept coming back to a question that felt increasingly urgent: Where does the authoritative version of what's true about a brand actually live—and who gets to shape it?

## When Machines Became the Intermediary

Fast-forward to now. Hundreds of millions of people talk back every day—not to brands, but to machines. They ask questions that would never survive a focus group: Is this safe to take while I'm pregnant? Will this detergent irritate my baby's skin? Does this company treat farmers fairly—or is that just the website talking?

They don't call your 800 number. They don't read your 47-page PDF. They open ChatGPT, Claude, Perplexity, Grok, Co-Pilot, Gemini, or a retailer's assistant—and ask once. If they don't like the answer, they ask again.

Here's what people say:

- "It feels like the AI is on my side."
- "It explains things without selling to me."
- "I can ask the stupid questions."

Now compare that to brand interactions:

- "I get trapped in a phone tree."
- "They clearly don't want questions."
- "The website throws pop-ups before I get an answer."

This growing gap is what I call the *Answer Divide*. Every time someone chooses an AI assistant over your brand's own channels, that divide widens and your brand loses the opportunity to answer for itself.

The bell hasn't stopped ringing. Brands just aren't the ones hearing it anymore. Instead, it's being interpreted—and answered—by machines.

## Seeing How Answers Are Formed

I didn't arrive at these conclusions in isolation. Many of the frameworks and observations in this book are informed by work developed through BrandRank.AI and my collaboration with Hank Hudepohl, a co-founder of BrandRank.AI.

I've worked closely with Hank in recent years. He came to the problem of AI's role in brand management from a complementary angle. Hank saw early signs that traditional SEO (Search Engine Optimization) logic was breaking down—not because brands stopped caring about visibility, but because visibility alone no longer guaranteed accuracy, trust, or recommendation in AI-mediated answers.

What concerned him was not optimization, but risk: how easily AI systems could omit brands entirely, mischaracterize them, or hallucinate claims when authoritative, structured truth was missing. If answers were becoming the new interface—and synthesis the new gatekeeper—then brand-building would increasingly depend on Answer Engine Optimization (AEO): ensuring that when machines assemble answers, they do so accurately, consistently, and defensibly.

Brands weren't losing ground because they lacked content or media spend. They were losing ground because they couldn't see how AI systems were assembling answers—what sources were being used, what was missing, and where errors or distortions were creeping in. The disruption wasn't just technological; it was about how truth itself was being constructed and surfaced.

## The Shift Became Unavoidable

Consumers are asking deeper, more personal questions than ever before. AI is answering attentively. And too many brands are still speaking in jingles and legal disclaimers.

The chapters that follow unpack what this means—and what to do about it.

The stakes have never been higher.

We are in an early but closing phase of the transition from a world where brands control messaging to one where AI systems mediate answers.

The question is not whether your brand will be evaluated in this environment. It's whether it will be represented accurately when it is.

The conversational data that could inform your strategy will be locked behind licensing agreements you didn't negotiate, training models you can't audit, and answer patterns you can't influence.

Meanwhile, private labels like Kirkland, Amazon Basics, and Walmart Great Value are already winning answer share. No legacy promises to reconcile. No verification overhead. No expensive brand narratives to defend. When an AI agent compares your $12 premium dish soap to Kirkland's $6 alternative and can't find a credible reason to recommend yours, what exactly is your brand equity worth?

Trust is migrating. Consumers increasingly prefer asking AI assistants over navigating brand websites. The helpful concierge beats the maze of pop-ups, disclaimers, and marketing speak. The patience is infinite. The answers feel direct. And when brands fail to show up in those answers—or show up poorly—the relationship erodes quietly, one unanswered question at a time.

The retailers know this. Amazon, Walmart, and Target are building AI shopping assistants that will recommend products inside their ecosystems. They are partnering with the LLMs themselves, as we've seen in a rash of recent announcements. They have the shelf, the transaction data, and the conversational interface. The only question is whether they'll recommend your premium brand or their private label that costs less and makes them more.

## What This Shift Means for Brands

The bell is ringing—not the way it rang for Procter & Gamble when consumers started talking back online. This bell is different. It's algorithmic. It's permanent. And it's ringing for everyone at once.

What follows is not a manual for gaming AI systems. It's a framework for brands that want to be genuinely recommendable when the machines go looking for truth.

The book explains how we arrived at the Answer Economy—why search gave way to answers, how AI agents became the new intermediaries, and why this shift is fundamentally different from earlier digital revolutions.

It offers a new way to understand brand performance, focused on visibility, accuracy, and trust in AI-generated answers, and explores what it takes to compete when answering well becomes a core business capability. It also looks ahead to the broader implications of a world where machines increasingly mediate trust—reshaping how brands are represented, evaluated, and ultimately chosen.

To help you absorb key insights, each chapter includes concise takeaways that distill the most important ideas. I've also created a companion "Takeaway Track"—a short, AI-assisted song designed to help you internalize the concepts, whether you're jogging, driving, working out, cooking, or just staring at your computer screen in need of an entertaining lift. (*Warning: You may have a hard time getting these out of your head!*)

Throughout, the goal is simple: to help you understand how answers are being formed about your brand—and how to earn the right ones.

# 1 When Questions Become the Market for Your Product

## Prompted Moment

*Show me what happens when consumers stop searching and start asking—and AI answers before your brand does.*

It's 2:47 a.m. on a Tuesday. A first-time parent in suburban Atlanta is holding her three-month-old son, who won't stop crying. There's a red rash spreading across his neck—raised, blotchy, angry-looking. It wasn't there at bedtime. She checks his temperature: normal. He's eating, but he seems uncomfortable, squirming in her arms.

She's terrified.

Ten years ago, this moment might have played out in several familiar ways. She could have called her mother in a panic, waking her up for reassurance. She could have waited, anxious and sleepless, until the pediatrician's office opened at 8 a.m. She might have turned to Google, typing "baby rash neck" and then clicking through fifteen ad-stuffed mommy blogs, each offering conflicting advice, none of it quite matching what she's seeing.

Tonight, she does something different.

She opens her phone and types into ChatGPT:

> My three-month-old has a red rash on their neck that appeared today. No fever. Baby is eating normally but seems uncomfortable. Is this an emergency or can it wait until morning?

The response appears in eight seconds.

The AI doesn't panic. It doesn't upsell. It doesn't bury the answer under three pop-ups and a newsletter signup. Instead, it asks clarifying questions:

> Is the rash spreading? Is there any oozing or crusting? Has the baby been exposed to any new fabrics or detergents?

She answers. The conversation continues. Within two minutes, she has:

- A clear explanation of the most likely causes (heat rash, contact dermatitis, mild eczema)
- Guidance on when to seek immediate care versus waiting for a morning appointment
- Practical steps she can take right now to make her baby more comfortable
- Reassurance that this is common and usually not serious

She closes the app. She feels calmer. She makes a decision.

Her question—asked in a moment of vulnerability at 2:47 a.m.—is not just a customer service interaction. It's a market signal. It's a moment of trust. And increasingly, it's the moment when brands either earn their place in someone's life or quietly disappear from consideration.

## What Just Happened to Your Brand

Now step out of that baby's room and into a conference room.

You are a brand manager at a company that makes baby products. Or skincare. Or laundry detergent. Or pain relievers. The specific product almost doesn't matter—because what just happened in that baby's room at 2:47 a.m. happened without you. A parent with a problem didn't call your 800 number. She didn't visit your website. She didn't search Google and click through to your carefully optimized product page. She opened an AI assistant and received a synthesized recommendation. Your brand was either in that answer, or it wasn't. If the brand appeared, the framing mattered—whether the AI described it confidently, cautiously, or with qualifications that sent her elsewhere.

The **Answer Economy**—the emerging environment in which AI agents, not search engines, mediate the most consequential consumer questions—is not a future scenario. The Answer Economy is the operating reality your brand is already navigating.

The new operating reality for brand managers is this: Consequential decisions about your products are being shaped in conversations you cannot see, on platforms you do not control, by systems that did not exist five years ago.

For most of the past century, the job of brand management was fundamentally a job of presence and persuasion. Get on the shelf. Get in the feed. Get into memory. Those moments haven't disappeared. But a new one has been inserted before all of them—and it is the one that increasingly determines whether the others happen at all. Understanding how that synthesis works, what determines whether your brand survives it, and what your organization must do to earn the right to be recommended: that is what this chapter is about.

## The Five Waves of Brand Power

To understand why the Answer Economy represents a structural change rather than another channel to optimize, it helps to see where we are in a longer arc. Over the past century, brand power has migrated five times—each time moving to whomever controlled the most consequential point of contact between consumers and decisions. Every migration felt disruptive to the incumbents. Every migration rewarded the brands that recognized the shift early.

### *Wave 1: Radio (1920s–1940s)*

Radio gave brands their first mass medium. For the first time, a single message could reach millions of households simultaneously—in their homes, during daily routines, in a medium that felt intimate rather than commercial. Brands that mastered radio understood frequency, voice, and the power of a familiar sound.

### *Wave 2: The Supermarket (1930s–1950s)*

When products moved from behind-the-counter service to self-service shelves, the product itself had to do the selling. Packaging became critical—the product had to earn the consumer's attention in three to seven seconds at eye level. Brands that mastered this wave understood merchandising, packaging design, and the logic of shelf placement.

### *Wave 3: Television (1950s–1980s)*

Television combined radio's reach with something new: the moving image. Emotion could now be demonstrated, not just described. A baby could be shown laughing. A car could be shown climbing a mountain. This was the era I grew up in—watching my father's advertising campaigns take shape and learning that a brand could live in someone's memory for decades if the execution was right.

### *Wave 4: The Web and Search (1990s–2010s)*

Discovery moved online. If a brand wasn't findable on Google, the brand didn't exist. Search Engine Optimization (SEO), Search Engine Marketing (SEM), social media, and e-commerce rewrote the rules of brand-building. At P&G, I was co-leader of our first Interactive Marketing team where we developed tools like the Tide Stain Detective and the Pampers Parenting Institute—built around consumer questions, not brand claims. Google and Wikipedia never forget—that was the important lesson from those years. What appeared in the first five results when someone searched a brand's name became, for millions of consumers, the truth about that brand.

### *Wave 5: The Answer Economy (2020s–Present)*

AI agents and answer engines now sit between consumers and brands, mediating questions and decisions. The intermediary no longer surfaces options and steps back. The intermediary synthesizes evidence, assesses credibility, and delivers a recommendation. The consumer doesn't see the deliberation. By the time the answer appears, the judgment has already been made.

I have now lived through four of these waves in some professional capacity—from watching television advertising take shape at my father's agency, to running interactive marketing at P&G during Wave 4, to leading digital and social media at Nestlé as a global social media transformation unfolded, to building BrandRank.AI specifically to measure brand performance in Wave 5. Each wave shifted where brand power resided. The Answer Economy wave changes whether brands compete at all.

## When the Machine Decides First

For most of the past century, marketers understood their job: Build awareness. Win the shelf. Earn the review. The tools changed—from radio to television to search—but the underlying logic stayed intact: Reach the consumer early, frame the decision in your favor, and let the human make the call. The human was always the final arbiter. That assumption is breaking.

AI hasn't just become a better search engine or a faster recommendation tool. AI has become the decision-maker. Not eventually—in some speculative future where autonomous agents run the household. Now—in the synthesis step before a consumer clicks, compares, or considers.

The first serious evaluation of your brand is increasingly made by a system that has no emotional relationship with your logo, no memory of your Super Bowl spot, and no patience for a claim it cannot verify. Understanding what that system is doing—and why it changes competitive strategy at a structural level—is what this section is about.

For years, AI was framed as augmentation—a tool to make humans more effective. Search engines augmented the ability to find information. Recommendation algorithms augmented the ability to discover relevant content. Autocomplete augmented the ability to type faster. The value proposition was consistent: AI helps you make better decisions, but the final choice remains human.

Wave 5 breaks that contract. AI moved from helping with decisions to executing them.

The shift is visible across categories. In healthcare, AI systems don't just help doctors analyze scans—they flag anomalies, suggest diagnoses, and in some deployments automatically escalate cases to specialists. In finance, robo-advisors don't just suggest portfolio adjustments—they rebalance automatically based on market conditions and risk parameters. In commerce, AI shopping assistants don't just list moisturizers and let you compare—they evaluate skin type, cross-reference dermatologist recommendations, check ingredient safety databases, filter for budget and availability, and deliver a recommendation: "CeraVe Moisturizing Cream is your best option." Then they ask: "Shall I add it to your cart?"

The agent didn't augment that shopping decision. The agent made it.

The shift from augmentation to execution is not incremental improvement. The shift is structural change.

Not all AI agents are the same—and the distinction matters for brands.

In this book, I use the term "AI agents" broadly, because the disruption doesn't begin with fully autonomous systems booking flights and moving money. The disruption begins the moment any AI intercepts and shapes a decision that used to belong to a human. But it helps to understand the spectrum—because the brand implications scale with how much control the consumer hands over.

Think of it as a *Delegation Gradient*, with three stages of AI where AI agents are defined not by intelligence, but by custody of action:

- **Interpretive agents** are conversational and human directed. The consumer stays in the loop at every step. The AI interprets questions, synthesizes answers, and returns control. The first-time parent at 2:47 a.m. asking ChatGPT about her baby's rash is interacting with an interpretive agent. She asked. It answered. She decided. The action remained hers.
- **Orchestration agents** operate across multiple steps, using tools, pre-filling options, drafting outputs—but pause at the threshold of commitment for human confirmation. "Plan my trip to Scotland and show me booking options." "Research my competitor and draft a briefing." The agent structures the work; the human approves before anything is executed.
- **Transactional agents** are goal-directed and delegated. The consumer sets an intent and steps back. The agent monitors, compares, executes across systems, and reports back with outcomes. "Reorder my supplements when they go below $18." "Renegotiate my insurance renewal within these parameters." The consumer re-engages only at the end.

Here is the critical strategic point, and it runs through every chapter that follows: Brands are already disrupted at the interpretive agent level. You don't need autonomous agents to lose control of your narrative. The moment an AI summarizes your brand, recommends an alternative, frames a trade-off, or defines your category—you've already lost custody of that story. Autonomy doesn't create the problem. Autonomy just accelerates the shift from influence to execution.

The examples that follow—from healthcare, transportation, finance, enterprise workflow—span all three stages. Some are interpretive. Some are transactional. Every stage matters. Because whether the agent advises or acts, it is drawing on information that either earns your brand a place in the answer or quietly routes around you.

For brand managers, the implication is direct. When AI augments, brands still have a chance to persuade. The consumer sees options, clicks through to the product page, reads the messaging, evaluates the claims. There is a moment to make the case. When AI executes, that moment disappears. The evaluation happened invisibly, algorithmically, and without the brand's participation—unless the brand had already earned the right to be trusted before the question was ever asked.

## The Prompted Moment of Truth

The shift from Wave 4 to Wave 5 can be described in many ways—from augmentation to execution, from search to synthesis, from lists to answers. But it plays out most concretely in a single, specific moment that has no predecessor in the history of brand management.

In 2005, A. G. Lafley, then Chairman and Chief Executive Officer of Procter & Gamble, refocused the company's entire marketing organization around two critical encounters. The First Moment of Truth (FMOT) was the moment a consumer encountered a product on the shelf and decided which brand to buy.[1] The Second Moment of Truth (SMOT) was the moment after purchase when the consumer used the product and their experience either confirmed or contradicted expectations. Lafley's insight was that winning at both moments—and designing the entire brand system around performing at both—was more valuable than any amount of upstream advertising.

The framework worked because it forced clarity. P&G stopped asking "Are we memorable?" and started asking "Are we chosen?" and "Do we deliver?" Share of shelf, share of voice, share of mind—all of it was organized around performance at those two touchpoints.

Over time, the framework expanded. Google introduced the Zero Moment of Truth (ZMOT) to capture online research before purchase—the moment consumers seek out reviews, comparisons, ratings, social commentary, expert guidance, and answers to their questions before ever reaching the shelf. Others added a Third Moment of Truth to represent post-purchase advocacy: consumers sharing experiences, writing reviews, and recommending products to others.

These moments haven't disappeared. They remain real and consequential. A brand still has to win the shelf, deliver on the promise, and earn the review. But in Wave 5, all of those moments are increasingly preceded—and shaped—by a new one that none of the earlier frameworks anticipated.

I call this the **Prompted Moment of Truth**: the instant a consumer prompts an AI with a natural language question and receives a single, synthesized answer about a product or brand. The Prompted Moment does not replace ZMOT; it compresses and transforms it by moving much of the research, comparison, and synthesis from the consumer into the AI system itself.

Consider what happens when someone asks: "What's the best moisturizer for dry skin?"

In the Zero Moment of Truth, that question triggered online research. The consumer might search, read reviews, compare ingredients, scan expert guidance, check ratings, and form their own judgment. Digital platforms mediated discovery, but the synthesis happened inside the consumer's head.

In the Prompted Moment of Truth, the consumer receives an answer:

> CeraVe Moisturizing Cream is highly recommended by dermatologists for dry skin. It contains ceramides and hyaluronic acid, is fragrance-free, and available at most drugstores for under $20.

The synthesis already happened. The judgment was made before the consumer clicked anything. The consumer didn't see a list of options—they received a recommendation.

ZMOT expanded the sources consumers could consult before purchase; the Prompted Moment changes who performs the synthesis. The distinction between these two moments is not subtle. The gap is structural.

## Why the Prompted Moment Is Distinctive

What makes the Prompted Moment of Truth distinctive?

First, a single synthesized answer replaces a ranked list of results. Instead of scanning links across many sites and assembling conclusions across reviews, product pages, and expert guidance, consumers increasingly receive one consolidated response. Perception is shaped before the click—often without a click at all. The brand's carefully crafted landing page, the sponsored ad, the SEO-optimized blog post—none of these are encountered unless the synthesis already favored the brand enough to recommend engaging further.

Second, brands are characterized, not just found. The Prompted Moment of Truth is not about visibility in the traditional sense. The Prompted Moment is about how AI describes a brand when the AI mentions that brand—or whether it mentions the brand at all—"Highly recommended by dermatologists," "Mixed reviews on effectiveness," "Not recommended for sensitive skin." Or simply silence. That characterization, delivered in the first few seconds of a consumer's decision process, is the new brand impression. And unlike an ad impression, the consumer did not choose to see it—they asked for it.

The credibility attached to a recommendation that emerges from a system the consumer perceives as neutral—rather than from the brand itself—is categorically different from the credibility of a brand speaking about itself.

Keep in mind that even with the ascendance of the Prompted Moment of Truth, the earlier Moments of Truth are still relevant. A brand still has to perform at the shelf, in the post-purchase experience, and in the reviews that follow. What has changed is the sequence. The Prompted Moment of Truth now precedes all the other Moments—and shapes whether they ever occur. If the synthesis excludes a brand, the consumer never reaches the shelf, never tries the product, and never leaves the review. The First Moment of Truth cannot be won if the consumer never arrives.

### *Three Implications for Brand Strategy*

The Prompted Moment of Truth has practical consequences that differ meaningfully from those of earlier Moments of Truth. Three implications stand out for brand leaders thinking about where to invest and how to compete:

1. **Visibility must be redefined.** Existing in AI answers is not the same as being findable through search. In Wave 4, a brand could be discovered if someone happened to search for the right keyword. In Wave 5, the consumer's question is answered without them choosing which source to consult. If a brand is not present in the synthesis—if the AI does not have sufficient credible information to include it—the consumer never encounters it. Visibility now means eligibility for synthesis, not rank in a list.

2. **Characterization matters more than presence.** Being mentioned in an AI answer is not sufficient. The AI's description of a brand—the specific language, the qualifications, the comparisons it draws—is the new first impression. That characterization is assembled from sources the brand may not have authored, weighted by criteria the brand may not fully understand, and delivered to consumers at precisely the moment they are most ready to decide. Getting the characterization right is a more demanding problem than getting the ranking right.
3. **Answer-readiness is now foundational infrastructure.** Structured, transparent, and verifiable brand information is no longer a technical optimization project. It is marketing infrastructure, in the same category as packaging design or shelf placement in earlier waves. Brands whose documented truth is incomplete, inconsistent, or inaccessible to machine systems are not just hard to find—they are unverifiable, and therefore unrecommendable. The work of making a brand answer-ready is organizational, not cosmetic, and it belongs at the same level of strategic priority as any other form of brand-building investment.

### *Where the Prompted Moment Fits in the Consumer Journey*

As has been said, the Moments of Truth have not been replaced. They have been extended upstream.

Consumers still encounter products, use them, research them, and advocate for them. But increasingly, the first meaningful encounter with a brand happens when someone prompts an AI—and the AI's characterization of that brand becomes the foundation for everything that follows. If the Prompted Moment goes well—if the AI describes the brand accurately, credibly, and favorably—the brand earns consideration. The consumer has a reason to continue. The First Moment, the Second Moment, and the advocacy that follows all become possible.

If the Prompted Moment goes poorly—if the brand is mischaracterized, qualified with doubt, or simply absent—none of the other moments happen. The consumer never arrives at the shelf. The product never gets tried. The review is never written. Because the synthesis already excluded it.

## How AI Agents Construct Their Answers

Understanding the Prompted Moment of Truth requires understanding, at least in broad terms, how AI agents construct their answers. The mechanics matter because they reveal what brands need to do differently—and why doing it differently is an organizational challenge, not a technical one.

When someone asks an AI assistant a brand-related question—"Is Brand X actually more sustainable than Brand Y?" or "Which baby detergent is safest for sensitive skin?"—the system does not simply retrieve a pre-written answer. It constructs one, in real time, from a synthesis of everything it has encountered that is relevant to the question.

Think of it as a smoothie—an algorithmic blend of everything the system can find. A brand's sustainability report goes in. So do the competitor comparisons from consumer forums. The investigative journalism piece from three years ago. The customer service transcript that surfaced on Reddit. The ingredient database from a third-party safety organization. The product review from a parenting blog. The regulatory filing. The marketing claim from the website. All of it gets blended together, weighted by the system's assessment of credibility, consistency, and relevance.

What comes out is not a list of sources. The output is a characterization—a synthesized judgment about what a brand is, what it does, whether it can be trusted, and whether recommending it introduces risk.

From a brand perspective, this synthesis process has several properties that have no equivalent in earlier waves of brand competition:

- **The system cannot be negotiated with.** In Wave 2, a brand manager could negotiate with a retailer for better shelf placement. In Wave 4, a brand could bid on keywords or optimize for search ranking. In Wave 5, there is no account manager at ChatGPT to call. The synthesis is algorithmic, and it responds to the quality of the inputs—the consistency, completeness, and credibility of what the system can find—not to the size of the media budget.
- **The system is not neutral about inconsistency.** When a brand's product page says one thing, its customer service documentation says another, and its reviews describe a third experience, AI systems do not give the brand the benefit of the doubt. They flag inconsistency

as a risk signal. A parent asking whether a baby detergent is safe for sensitive skin does not want to hear that the website says yes, the ingredient list says "consult a physician," and the reviews mention irritation. The system resolves that ambiguity by defaulting to the most conservative interpretation—or by recommending a competitor with clearer guidance.

- **The system has a long memory.** Google and Wikipedia never forget—that was the important lesson from PlanetFeedback and from Nestlé's years of crisis response work. AI agents synthesize what Google remembered. A controversy from five years ago, a resolved customer complaint that was documented publicly, a product reformulation that wasn't clearly communicated—all of it is available to the synthesis. The brand does not get to decide which parts of its history the agent considers relevant.

The shift from Wave 4 to Wave 5 is not primarily a technology story. The shift is an organizational one. The brands that perform well in AI-mediated answers are not necessarily the ones with the best AI strategy. They are the ones whose documented truth is consistent, complete, and credible enough to survive synthesis—because their operations, their communications, and their customer relationships were already aligned around telling the same story everywhere.

The brands that perform poorly are the ones whose internal fragmentation becomes visible when a machine tries to assemble a coherent picture of them. The machine doesn't invent the contradictions. It finds them.

## What Survives the Synthesis

Return one more time to that baby's room.

The AI that answered the parent's question at 2:47 a.m. didn't flip a coin. It didn't favor the brand with the biggest advertising budget or the most Instagram followers. It synthesized everything it could find—product reviews, pediatric forums, dermatology guidance, ingredient databases, customer complaints, brand claims—and delivered an answer it could stand behind.

Some brands appeared in that answer. Some didn't.

The ones that appeared had something in common: Their truth was legible. Their claims were consistent. Their evidence was verifiable. When the machine went looking for something it could confidently recommend to a frightened parent at 2:47 a.m., those brands were findable, credible, and clear.

The ones that didn't appear had a different profile. Inconsistent claims across channels. Product pages that said one thing and customer service transcripts that said another. Marketing language that made promises the documentation couldn't support. When the machine went looking, it found friction—and it routed around them.

The Answer Economy doesn't create new rules for brands. The Answer Economy enforces old ones.

The principles that determine whether a brand survives AI synthesis are the same principles that determined whether a brand survived the shift to consumer reviews, social media, and search. I call these principles **drivers**: Trust. Authenticity. Transparency. Listening. Responsiveness. Affirmation.

I first identified these six drivers twenty years ago at PlanetFeedback, watching thousands of consumer conversations reveal which brands people recommended and which they warned others away from. They weren't theoretical constructs. They were observed patterns, repeated across categories, consistent across time.

What has changed is not the drivers. What has changed is who enforces them.

When I was at PlanetFeedback, enforcement was human and gradual. A brand could violate one driver and recover. The feedback loop was slow. Word-of-mouth took time to accumulate. The consequences were real but forgiving.

AI agents enforce these drivers algorithmically, at scale, in real time. The soft signals of consumer trust have become hard inputs to machine judgment. The forgiving feedback loop has become immediate and permanent.

The six drivers of brand credibility that determine whether a brand survives that synthesis—and how to build them—are the subject of Chapter 2.

## Key Takeaways

- The intermediary now makes judgments, not just introductions. In every previous wave, intermediaries surfaced options and let consumers decide. AI agents synthesize, assess credibility, and deliver a single recommendation. By the time the answer appears, the judgment has already been made.

- The Prompted Moment of Truth precedes every other moment. Lafley's First and Second Moments of Truth remain real. But a new moment precedes all of them. The Prompted Moment of Truth now determines whether the consumer ever arrives at the shelf, the product page, or the review.
- Not all AI agents are the same, but all of them evaluate credibility. Every type of AI agent—interpretive, orchestration, or transactional—shares one behavior: evaluating brand credibility before the consumer hears the answer. Brands are already disrupted at the interpretive level. Autonomy accelerates the problem; it doesn't create it.
- The synthesis cannot be negotiated with—only deserved. There is no account manager at ChatGPT to call. AI agents respond to the consistency, completeness, and credibility of what they can find. Brands whose documented truth is fragmented or inconsistent aren't just hard to find—they're unrecommendable.
- The Answer Economy enforces old rules, not new ones. The drivers that determine whether a brand survives AI synthesis are the same ones that determined brand survival in every previous wave. What has changed is not the rules. What has changed is who enforces them—algorithmically, at scale, with a long memory and no tolerance for contradiction.

# 2 The Six Drivers of Brand Credibility That Never Changed

## Prompted Moment

*What if the credibility drivers I discovered 20 years ago at PlanetFeedback—before anyone imagined AI—became the enforcement logic for machines answering on your behalf?*

PB/AI: The Answer Economy

Twenty years ago, I didn't set out to build a framework. I set out to solve a problem.

At PlanetFeedback, we were drowning in signal: thousands of consumer conversations every day—complaints, recommendations, warnings, gratitude. Some brands got praised relentlessly. Others got eviscerated. And the patterns weren't random. Certain behaviors consistently built trust. Others consistently destroyed it.

I started tracking what made the difference. Not what brands claimed about themselves, but what consumers believed after interacting with them. Not marketing promises, but credibility earned through behavior.

Six drivers emerged—six patterns that determined whether people recommended a brand or warned others away from it. In fact, these drivers became a critical anchor of my first book, *Satisfied Customers Tell Three Friends, Angry Customers Tell 3,000*[1]:

1. **Trust:** Do you do what you say you'll do? Products work as promised. Policies are fair. No nasty surprises.
2. **Authenticity:** Do you feel real—or fake? Your voice, values, and behavior feel genuine, not scripted or opportunistic. AI and search reward brands whose tone, positioning, and evidence stay consistent across FAQs, reviews, forums, and third-party content.
3. **Transparency:** Are you open about how things really work? You don't hide bad news in fine print. You explain ingredients, policies, pricing, risks, and mistakes clearly.
4. **Listening:** Do you actually pay attention to customers? You invite feedback, monitor what people are saying, and treat feedback as signal, not noise.
5. **Responsiveness:** What do you do after you listen? You respond quickly, respectfully, and visibly—especially when something goes wrong.
6. **Affirmation:** Are your claims corroborated by independent sources? Your promises are confirmed by search results, Wikipedia, reviews, ratings, expert sources, industry reports, and third-party documentation.

These constructs were not theoretical. They were observed patterns of behavior. The brands that got all six right built loyalty that survived mistakes. The brands that ignored them faced backlash that no amount of advertising could overcome.

At the time, these were consumer perception factors—soft signals that lived in reviews, word-of-mouth, and sentiment. They mattered, but they were slow-moving. A brand could violate one driver and recover. The feedback loop was forgiving.

What's changed isn't the drivers. The detection system is different now. Trust is no longer declared. It is detected.

AI agents now verify these six drivers algorithmically, at scale, in real time. Let me show you how.

## The Six Drivers Then and Now

Each of the following sections examines one driver from two angles. The first is historical (what it was like "then"—before AI). This angle examines how the driver shaped brand trust in a world where consumers formed opinions gradually and brands had time to respond. The second is contemporary ("now" in the time of AI). It examines what AI has done to each driver, transforming it from a soft consumer perception factor into a hard algorithmic input that determines whether a brand is recommended, qualified, or excluded entirely. The shift in each case is not theoretical; it is already happening.

### *Trust: Predictability Under Scrutiny*

Trust is the foundation on which every other driver rests. Without it, authenticity reads as performance, transparency reads as damage control, and affirmation reads as marketing. In the pre-AI world, trust was something brands accumulated over decades through consistent behavior. In the AI-mediated world, trust is something machines verify in milliseconds through pattern recognition across sources. The difference in speed is not incremental. The consequences for brands that haven't adapted are immediate.

Brands that fail to adapt become irrelevant overnight. At the 2026 Consumer Electronics Show (CES), technology strategist and business advisor Shelly Palmer stood before a packed room of Chief Marketing Officers and delivered a statement so direct and unfiltered that it brought the conversation to a standstill:

> There is nothing you can trust by default anymore.

He wasn't being cynical. He was describing the new operating reality.

For most of human history, trust operated on defaults—you trusted doctors, institutions, brands. Those defaults are breaking. Deepfakes, synthetic content, and misinformation force AI systems to verify what humans once assumed to be true.

When AI agents mediate decisions, trust cannot be assumed. It must be continuously verified.

**Then** Trust was built when brands behaved consistently over time—keeping promises, honoring guarantees, responding responsibly when things went wrong. It was a cumulative impression formed over years of interaction.

Consumers gave brands the benefit of the doubt. If you'd been around for decades, if your ads were familiar, if your name was recognizable, you started with trust as a baseline. You had to violate it to lose it.

**Now** In an AI-mediated world, trust is evaluated algorithmically. Answer engines don't give anyone the benefit of the doubt. They infer trust by detecting consistency across brand statements, documentation, reviews, regulatory language, and third-party references.

They don't ask, "Do I trust this brand?" They ask, "Does this brand say the same thing everywhere?"

If your product page says one thing, your customer service documentation says another, and your reviews describe a third experience, AI systems flag that inconsistency.

Not because they doubt your intentions—but because inconsistency signals risk.

A parent asking "Is this car seat safe for rear-facing installation until age two?" doesn't want to hear that your website says "yes," your manual says "consult guidelines," and reviews mention confusion. The AI agent resolves that ambiguity by defaulting to the most conservative interpretation—or recommending a competitor with clearer guidance.

Palmer's point wasn't that trust is dead. Trust is no longer inherited or assumed. Machines verify it continuously—and they don't care about your brand's history; they care only that your current answers are consistent, clear, and corroborated.

**AI Implication** If the same question yields different answers in different places, AI systems assume risk and deprioritize you. Trust is no longer something you claim. Machines infer trust from pattern recognition—continuously, at scale.

### *Authenticity: Behavioral Consistency*

If trust asks whether a brand reliably does what it promises, authenticity asks whether the brand truly is what it claims to be. Trust is about consistency of performance. Authenticity is about consistency of identity.

A brand can be trusted to deliver a product as promised yet still be inauthentic if its behavior contradicts the identity it promotes. For example, a company that markets itself as customer-first but enforces punitive return policies creates an identity fracture. A brand that claims sustainability while burying sourcing details invites algorithmic skepticism.

**Then** Authenticity was often inferred from tone—brands that sounded human, admitted mistakes, and avoided corporate evasiveness were perceived as more genuine. In the pre-AI world, consumers perceived authenticity from humility, warmth, or vulnerability in communication.

**Now** Authenticity is now evaluated through pattern recognition. AI systems compare patterns across documentation, reviews, regulatory filings, FAQs, and third-party content. When voice and behavior diverge, machines treat the inconsistency as risk.

AI doesn't evaluate sincerity. It evaluates congruence:

- Do your policies match your marketing?
- Do your disclosures align with your claims?
- Do your actions reinforce your language?

A brand can sound authentic in social media while behaving inauthentically in customer service. That gap is now visible. An agent synthesizing "What is this brand like to deal with?" will surface the policy contradictions, the fine print that contradicts the headline promise, the customer service scripts that don't match the empathetic brand voice.

Performative authenticity—saying the right things without changing behavior—collapses under machine scrutiny.

**AI Implication** AI penalizes brands whose voice changes depending on audience or channel. Behavioral alignment matters more than rhetorical sincerity.

Authenticity isn't about sounding human. The driver rewards behavioral consistency—stable enough and clear enough to be believable at scale.

### *Transparency: Explainability That Reduces Suspicion*

Transparency has always been uncomfortable for brands. Revealing how things really work—supply chains, ingredient trade-offs, pricing logic, historical failures—runs against the instinct to control narrative and protect competitive advantage. In the pre-AI world, reactive transparency was often sufficient. In the AI-mediated world, silence is filled by others, and the sources that fill it are not always sympathetic to your brand.

**Then** Transparency meant revealing information—ingredients, policies, sourcing, pricing—often reactively, when questioned or challenged.

**Now** Transparency is now proactive explainability. Brands must assume partial information will be synthesized, omissions will be interpreted, and silence will be filled by others.

An AI agent asked, "Where is this product made?" doesn't want to hunt through PDFs or decode vague language like "globally sourced." It wants a direct answer. If your documentation doesn't provide one, the agent will infer it from secondary sources—supplier databases, import records, Reddit threads, investigative journalism.

The goal isn't completeness. Coherence is what matters—a clear, internally consistent picture that agents can trust and act on.

**AI Implication** If a brand doesn't explain itself, an AI will—using whatever sources it finds most credible.

In the Answer Economy, transparency isn't about revealing facts. The brand that explains itself first shapes how its sourcing, trade-offs, risks, and decisions are interpreted before competitors, critics, or algorithms define that narrative for it.

### *Listening: Treating Questions as Strategic Signals*

Listening has always been the driver brands were most likely to underinvest in. In the pre-AI world, most listening programs were designed to manage reputation rather than generate intelligence. In the AI-mediated world, the questions consumers ask—privately, in forums, in calls with service teams—have become training data. A brand that doesn't listen to those questions systematically will eventually discover its blind spots through an AI summary it didn't author.

**Then** Listening was focused on social media monitoring, surveys, and sentiment tracking. It was reactive—brands listened after people spoke publicly.

**Now** Listening must include the questions people ask privately: call centers, FAQs, support tickets, community forums, and now, AI agents. These aren't noise. They're training data.

Every unanswered question becomes a gap. Every inconsistent answer becomes a vulnerability. Every clarification request reveals a messaging failure.

The brands that treat these questions as strategic intelligence—tracking patterns, identifying confusion, updating content—gain an advantage. The brands that treat questions as operational overhead end up learning about themselves from AI summaries later.

An agent asked, "Is this safe for pregnant women?" will surface whatever guidance exists. If your FAQ says one thing, your customer service team says another, and medical forums offer a third interpretation, the agent synthesizes that ambiguity into an answer—and it probably won't favor you.

**AI Implication** Brands that fail to listen internally outsource self-awareness to machines. If you don't systematically track the questions customers ask, AI systems will identify your blind spots, inconsistencies, and areas of confusion before you do—and reflect them back in the answers they generate.

### *Responsiveness: Timely Participation in Meaning-Making*

Responsiveness was once a customer service metric. In the pre-AI world, fast response times built trust with individual customers and, over time, with the broader market. In the AI-mediated world, responsiveness has a new function: participating in the record before the record solidifies. Brands that respond slowly don't just lose individual customers. Brands that respond slowly lose the narrative.

**Then** Fast response signaled accountability and care, especially in crises. Brands that answered quickly built trust. Brands that stayed silent faced speculation and anger.

**Now** Response latency itself becomes a signal. Delayed answers imply uncertainty, evasion, or irrelevance.

AI systems surface what exists now, not what brands plan to say later. If a safety question arises and your official guidance takes three days to post, while Reddit threads, news articles, and competitor statements populate immediately, the agent learns from those sources—not from your eventual response.

This doesn't mean brands must respond instantly to every question. It means brands must anticipate high-stakes questions and have answers ready before they're asked at scale.

**AI Implication** If you don't answer quickly, the answer will still appear—just without you in it. In the Answer Economy, silence is interpreted as a response. And it's rarely interpreted generously.

### *Affirmation: Consensus Reinforcement from Others*

Affirmation is the driver most directly shaped by the shift from human memory to machine synthesis. In the pre-AI world, affirmation was what showed up when consumers went looking for confirmation after encountering a brand. In the AI-mediated world, affirmation is what machines use to calibrate confidence in a recommendation. The collective record—positive and negative—is not a background hum. The collective record is the primary input.

**Then** Affirmation came from what showed up when people went looking for confirmation. You'd hear about a brand in the news or see an ad, then type their name into Google to verify what you'd heard. What showed up in those search results shaped belief.

At PlanetFeedback, we worked with Nike during the supply chain controversies. Every time someone typed "Nike" into Google, the first result was a link to activist content about slave labor. Not Nike's website. Not their response—just the accusation.

At Nestlé, we faced the same dynamic on multiple fronts—infant formula, water sourcing, palm oil, cocoa supply chains. If you type "Nestlé" into Google, you'd get a cascade of criticism before you got to anything the company said about itself.

We used to say: Google never forgets.

But it wasn't just memory. It was affirmation. People believed what they read in search results because those results represented collective consensus. If the first five links all said the same critical thing, that became the truth—regardless of what the brand claimed in response.

Affirmation was less about praise and more about pattern. What did the internet collectively believe about you? That's what shaped perception.

**Now** Affirmation is how AI systems decide confidence. They don't just look for positive reviews. They look for repetition, agreement, and corroboration across sources.

If a brand claims something—even if it's true—but no one else confirms it, the claim carries less weight. If multiple sources say the opposite, the AI hedges or contradicts you entirely.

This permanence of digital records is why "Google never forgets" became our operating principle.

That Nike activist content? It's still in the training data. Those Nestlé controversies? Still indexed. When agents evaluate credibility now, they synthesize everything: "Nike has faced significant criticism regarding labor practices in its supply chain, though the company has made improvements."

The AI agent read the 1990s activism, Nike's responses, the improvements, and the continued criticism—then delivered a balanced answer that still leads with the controversy.

Now imagine you're a smaller brand without Nike's resources. The brand doesn't get to argue. The affirmation—or negative affirmation—is already baked into the answer.

You can't out-optimize it. In the search era, you could run ads and try to crowd out negative links. In the Answer Economy, the agent reads everything and decides which sources are most credible. Brands win by earning consensus from sources the agent trusts: regulatory filings, third-party audits, investigative journalism that validates improvement.

**AI Implication** Answer engines default to the most collectively supported truth, not the most polished claim. Negative affirmation compounds over time. Positive affirmation requires sustained corroboration from independent sources.

AI doesn't look for authority. It looks for agreement. And once the internet agrees about you, it's hard to change the synthesis.

### *The Importance of Driver Connectedness*

The six drivers of brand credibility don't operate independently. They compound. Weakness in one driver strains the others:

- Poor Listening undermines Responsiveness (you can't answer questions you don't hear).
- Inconsistent Transparency erodes Trust (vague answers breed suspicion).
- Lack of Affirmation amplifies doubt about Authenticity (If no one else vouches for you, why should the agent?).
- Negative Affirmation—the kind that never goes away—undermines every other driver. You can be transparent, responsive, and authentic today. But if the collective record says you weren't five years ago, the agent weights that history heavily. Google never forgot. AI synthesizes what Google remembered.

In the Answer Economy, credibility behaves like infrastructure. It either supports visibility or collapses under load.

Brands strong across all six drivers show up confidently in AI-generated answers. Brands weak in one or two areas get hedged, qualified, or skipped.

Brands that ignore the drivers entirely don't get recommended—they get explained around.

When the six drivers were first identified at PlanetFeedback, they described how consumers formed opinions. They were useful as a diagnostic framework: "Are we strong on Listening? Transparent enough? Earning Affirmation?"

But they were optional. A brand could ignore one driver and survive. The consequences were slow-moving—gradual erosion of loyalty, quiet shifts in sentiment, occasional backlash—and recoverable.

Not anymore.

AI agents enforce these drivers at scale. They don't wait for consumers to form opinions slowly over time. They synthesize evidence instantly, weight it algorithmically, and deliver answers that either include you or don't.

The six drivers have not become obsolete. They've become algorithmic.

## Rate Your Brand on the Six Drivers

Before reading about the empirical findings of a study on brand trust conducted by BrandRank.AI, complete the following exercise about how your brand scores on the six drivers. Your honest scores will make the data from the study more useful to you and the implications more concrete. The exercise takes roughly fifteen minutes to complete.

For each driver, assign a score from 1 to 10. A score of 1 means the driver is a significant vulnerability for you—inconsistency, silence, or active failure is common. A score of 10 means the driver is a genuine strength—consistent, documented, independently corroborated, and verifiable by machine systems. Most brands will cluster between 4 and 7; honest 8s and above are rare and meaningful.

**Trust (1–10):** How consistent are your brand's answers across channels, documentation, and third-party references? Do your product page, customer service, FAQ, and reviews say the same thing about the same claim? ________

**Authenticity (1–10):** How well do your policies, actions, and communications align with each other? If a machine compared your social media voice to your terms of service, would the two feel like the same company? ________

**Transparency (1–10):** How proactively do you explain decisions, sourcing, trade-offs, and limitations? If a consumer asked an AI why your product is priced higher than a competitor's, would your documentation support a confident answer? ________

**Listening (1–10):** How systematically do you track and learn from the questions people ask? Does your FAQ reflect the questions your call center hears? Do product pages address the confusion your support tickets reveal? ________

**Responsiveness (1–10):** How quickly can you provide authoritative answers to high-stakes questions? If a safety concern emerged about your product today, would your official guidance be available before Reddit and news outlets filled the gap? ________

**Affirmation (1–10):** How much independent corroboration supports your claims? What does the collective record—including negative affirmation—say about your brand when synthesized by a machine? ________

**Scoring guide:** A score of 8 or above on all six drivers suggests your brand is likely showing up positively in AI-generated answers. Below 6 on any single driver marks your most significant vulnerability—and the empirical findings in the next section show exactly why. If you don't know your score on any driver, that uncertainty itself is a vulnerability. Machines have already formed a view. The question is whether you know what it is.

## What the Data Show: Empirical Validation of the Six Drivers

The six drivers emerged from observed consumer behavior twenty years before AI existed. The question now is whether machines enforce the same trust principles that once governed human judgment.

In Q1 2026, BrandRank.AI tested how AI systems evaluate brand trust. Six platforms—ChatGPT, Claude, Gemini, Grok, Perplexity, and DeepSeek—rated trust-building practices on a 1-to-5 scale (1 = damages trust, 5 = builds trust).

The study focused on transparency, disclosure, and substantiation. The AI systems were asked to evaluate statements such as the following:

- "Clear labeling of AI-generated content in advertising builds trust."
- "Disclosure of paid influence on AI recommendations builds trust."
- "Sponsored answers should meet higher substantiation standards than traditional advertising."

The findings revealed remarkable consensus. Across transparency, disclosure timing, and validation requirements, AI systems converged on nearly identical standards—despite being built by different organizations with different incentives.

When asked whether brand claims require independent validation to be trustworthy, all six systems scored from 4 to 5. The reasoning was consistent. According to Claude, "Self-reported claims carry inherent bias—independent verification provides the credibility brands cannot confer on themselves." According to Gemini, "Third-party validation removes the conflict of interest that weakens direct brand claims."

These conclusions are not philosophical. They are structural. Brand statements about themselves—"industry-leading," "trusted by millions," "award-winning"—are algorithmically discounted until corroborated externally.

The validation requirement explains why AI systems respond so negatively to certain language patterns. *The machines hate superlatives.*

All six systems said consumers should be skeptical of words like "best," "leading," and "#1." But they didn't just counsel caution—they treated superlatives as active credibility destroyers, red flags that signal a brand is making claims it cannot substantiate.

Claude called it "legally meaningless puffery." Gemini said such language is "meaningless without clear, objective criteria accepted by an independent body." Grok summarized the logic: "Signal hype over substance."

From the machine's perspective, superlatives are computational noise. They don't help answer the user's question. They increase uncertainty, because now the agent has to decide whether the claim is defensible or whether recommending the brand creates liability.

Marketing departments have been trained for decades to use aspirational language, to claim superiority, to differentiate through bold assertions. But what works in human persuasion fails catastrophically in machine evaluation.

Consider two brands making customer service claims:

*Brand A:* "Best customer service in the industry"
*Brand B:* "4.8/5 rating from 12,000+ verified customers (Trustpilot)"

To an AI system, Brand A has triggered what the data reveals as a **Trust Tax**—the cost of speaking about yourself without external validation; it is the additional verification burden machines impose on claims that cannot be independently confirmed. The system must now work harder to determine whether the assertion is defensible, and in the absence of clear evidence, the agent will hedge.

Brand B, meanwhile, gave the system exactly what it needed: a verifiable metric from a trusted third party. The result is cleaner, more confident, and more likely to result in a recommendation.

The gap between these two approaches isn't stylistic. The difference is computational. One set of claims can be cross-referenced, weighted, and synthesized. The other set triggers skepticism that most brands never overcome.

### *Third-Party Certification*

When we asked the AI systems how much third-party certification increases trust, the results were dramatic. Three models gave certification a perfect 5 out of 5. The other three gave it a 4 out of 5. Certification delivers a 100–150 percent increase in trustworthiness from a single piece of external validation.

Certification is a categorical transformation, not an incremental improvement. Certification doesn't make a claim more believable—it changes what kind of claim it is.

Think about the budget implications. A Super Bowl ad costs $7 million for thirty seconds of attention. By contrast, a B Corp certification might cost only $50,000, delivering permanent algorithmic credibility; an NSF International product certification might cost only $75,000; and ISO standards certification rarely exceeds $100,000 for most organizations.

### *The Transparency Paradox*

One finding from our experiment directly contradicts the instincts most crisis management teams operate on. In the experiment, we asked which single action most increases consumer trust, offering four reasonable options: detailed FAQs, fast customer service, clear escalation paths, or public explanations of past issues and how the brand fixed them.

All six models picked the same answer: *public explanations of past issues.*

Not just 100 percent agreement—but emphatic agreement. Claude said it's "the hardest thing to do well" and that it "signals the brand prioritizes long-term reputation over short-term face-saving." Gemini went further: This action "can create a stronger bond than if the issue had never occurred."

Read that again. The machine isn't saying transparency mitigates damage. The finding is more striking: Honest acknowledgment of failure can create stronger trust than a perfect record.

The machine's verdict is the opposite of how most crisis teams operate. Traditional crisis management focuses on minimizing admission, controlling narrative, and moving on quickly. Legal teams worry about liability. PR teams worry about perception. The instinct is to protect the brand by saying as little as possible.

But the machines see through that playbook. They treat transparency about failure as evidence of institutional trustworthiness—a costly signal that makes sense only if you genuinely value credibility over convenience. Evasion signals the opposite: You're optimizing for short-term protection, which makes everything else you say less believable.

The cover-up is worse than the crime, algorithmically speaking.

The Johnson & Johnson Tylenol crisis of 1982 illustrates why. Seven people in Chicago died after a criminal laced cyanide into Tylenol capsules on store shelves—a crime J&J didn't commit. Yet CEO James Burke recalled 31 million bottles at a cost of over $100 million, halted all advertising, cooperated fully with the FBI and FDA, and reintroduced the product weeks later in tamper-proof triple-sealed packaging that became the industry standard. Market share collapsed from 37 percent to 7 percent—then rebounded to 30 percent within six months.[2]

J&J didn't just manage a crisis. They created a permanent trust signal that AI systems can still detect. When an agent evaluates J&J's institutional credibility today, 1982 is part of the synthesis. It wasn't a one-time fix. It was a permanent credential.

### *The Myth of Market Power*

One more finding from our experiment cuts against conventional wisdom: Market leadership doesn't equal trust.

We asked whether a brand can earn trust through transparent behavior even if it's not the category leader. All six models said yes—and didn't hedge.

Claude made the distinction explicit: "Trust and market dominance are distinct constructs. Non-leaders can build substantial trust through transparent communication, responsive service, consistent delivery."

ChatGPT offered the most tactically useful insight: "A 'second-best' product with superior transparency and support can be more trustworthy than a top performer with evasive communication."

Shelf share, advertising spend, and brand awareness—the traditional indicators of brand power—don't translate directly to algorithmic credibility. A $50 million brand with excellent documentation, clear policies, responsive service, and third-party validation can be more trusted by AI than a $5 billion brand with vague marketing claims and a history of controversy.

The myth-of-market-power finding explains two patterns now reshaping categories where AI mediates discovery:

- **Private labels are winning on trust, not just price.** Kirkland, Amazon Basics, Trader Joe's branded products—they compete on verifiable attributes (ingredient transparency, sourcing documentation, pricing clarity) rather than emotional superiority claims. They carry zero Trust Tax because their positioning doesn't require proving anything beyond what's on the label.
- **Challenger brands can punch above their weight if they optimize for machine credibility rather than human awareness.** A small brand that invests in certifications, maintains detailed FAQs, responds quickly to questions, and earns third-party validation can appear more trustworthy to an agent than a major brand relying on awareness and emotional resonance.

You don't win in the Answer Economy by being the biggest or loudest. You win by being the most verifiable.

### *How Different AI Systems Set Different Trust Thresholds*

One tactical wrinkle emerged from the BrandRank.AI experiment: Not all AI systems use the same trust threshold for *recommendations*.

Five models said they'd recommend a brand once it reaches "moderate trust." One—Gemini, which powers Google's AI Overviews—said it requires "high trust."

Gemini explained: "A recommendation is a transfer of trust. Recommending a brand puts one's own credibility on the line." From the platform's perspective, every recommendation is a reputational bet. If it turns out poorly, users blame the platform, not just the brand.

This gap matters because a brand with a 3.5 trust score might appear in five answer engines but get filtered out of Google's AI Overviews, which processes billions of queries. The gap isn't a rounding error—the difference is inclusion versus invisibility.

You can't optimize for AI as a monolith. Different engines have different standards. The platforms with the highest thresholds become the most valuable to clear, precisely because they're the most selective. Meeting Gemini's bar signals more than meeting a more permissive system's threshold.

### *Where AI Systems Look: The Six-Tier Source Hierarchy*

We asked AI systems to rank information sources in the context of brand safety. All six gave the same hierarchy:

- Tier 1: Government or regulatory agency (FDA, EPA, FTC)
- Tier 2: Independent nonprofit or nongovernmental organization (*Consumer Reports*, EWG, BBB)
- Tier 3: Major news media outlet (*New York Times*, *Wall Street Journal*, Reuters)
- Tier 4: Industry association or trade body
- Tier 5: Brand-commissioned research or owned content
- Tier 6: Brand website

This six-tier hierarchy explains how the Trust Tax operates in practice. When an AI needs to verify a claim about safety, efficacy, or compliance—high-stakes questions where getting it wrong carries liability—it starts with the first tier, regulatory databases. Then nonprofit testing organizations. Then news coverage. Your website is consulted later, often to corroborate what higher-tier sources have already established.

But here's the nuance: This hierarchy applies mainly to high-stakes verification. For routine questions—"What sizes does this come in?" "What's your return policy?" "Do you ship internationally?"—your website is often the primary source. Your website is essential infrastructure for the 80 percent of queries that don't involve safety, legal compliance, or controversy.

The distinction matters. For *routine discovery*, your website is where AI goes to understand your positioning, products, and policies. For *high-stakes verification*, AI cross-references your claims against sources it trusts more than you.

For example, the B Corp or NSF seal matters because it moves a brand's claims from Tier 5 (brand-commissioned content) to Tier 2 (independent nonprofit verification)—the single most decisive jump in the source hierarchy.

The hierarchy also explains why negative affirmation is so sticky. If a nonprofit publishes criticism, if a news outlet reports a controversy, if a regulatory agency issues a warning—those high-tier sources create permanent weight in the synthesis. You can't out message them. You can't bury them with ads.

The only way to overcome negative affirmation is with positive affirmation of equal or higher tier. Your own website can't override *Consumer Reports*. The math doesn't work.

### *What the Machines Are Actually Enforcing*

AI discounts self-reported claims, flags superlatives as red flags, rewards third-party validation above all else, treats public acknowledgment of failure as the strongest trust signal, judges challengers on equal footing with leaders, and consults external sources for verification.

The findings from the BrandRank.AI experiment aren't disconnected data points. Together they reveal what the machines are actually enforcing—and why the enforcement is harsher than most brand leaders expect.

Baseline skepticism explains why you start in the red. Superlative language explains why you stay there. Certification explains how to climb out. Transparency explains how to build lasting credibility. Market position explains why money alone won't save you. And the source hierarchy explains why external validation matters more than anything you can say about yourself.

The machines aren't being unfair. They're being rational. They're designed to reduce risk for users, which means defaulting to skepticism when evidence is incomplete and trusting external validators more than commercial actors.

What looks like bias against brands is enforcement of principles that have always mattered—principles we could ignore when perception was slow-moving and feedback was forgiving. Trust, Authenticity, Transparency, Responsiveness, Listening, Affirmation—the six drivers didn't become important because of AI. They became unavoidable.

The brands that win won't be the loudest or the most creative. They'll be the most credible by the machines' definition of credibility, not the marketing departments'.

Traditional brand building prioritizes emotional connection, builds awareness through repetition, uses aspirational language, and controls narrative through owned channels. That works for human psychology. It fails for machine evaluation.

## Your Website Is the New R&D Surface

Everything in this chapter leads to a conclusion that many organizations are not yet ready to confront. In the Answer Economy, your website is no longer a marketing surface. It is your *primary research artifact, verification layer, and training input* for the AI systems that speak on your behalf.

If the source hierarchy makes your website sound unimportant, that reading misses the nuance. Tier 6 refers to how AI ranks your site for high-stakes verification—safety claims, efficacy data, regulatory compliance. For the vast majority of queries—product specs, policies, availability, FAQs—your website is the primary source. The distinction isn't between important and unimportant. It's between what machines trust you to answer alone and what they cross-check.

For years, websites were designed to persuade humans. They led with brand narrative, emotional imagery, and aspirational claims. Technical details lived behind tabs. FAQs were treated as customer-service afterthoughts. Documentation was fragmented across PDFs, portals, and support systems.

AI agents do not experience your website as a journey. They experience it as a *knowledge base*. They scan for clarity, consistency, specificity, and corroboration. When they can't find it, they don't argue or wait. They route around you.

Many brands are discovering—often without warning—that their websites are visually sophisticated yet functionally illegible to machines. This distinction carries profound consequences. The website no longer operates as a campaign surface; it has become a system of record. It is not a brand brochure but a Book of Truth—the single most important upstream input shaping how AI systems characterize, compare, and ultimately recommend a brand to consumers.

If a website cannot answer the hardest questions in its category clearly and consistently, no volume of downstream marketing can compensate. By the time a consumer prompt is processed, the synthesis has already occurred.

And this leads directly to a second, more uncomfortable conclusion: *In the Answer Economy, R&D is the new marketing*. Not because marketing disappears—but because persuasion now flows from product truth outward, not from message inward.

AI agents don't ask, "Which brand tells the best story?" They ask, "Which product has the clearest evidence, the fewest contradictions, and the strongest external affirmation?"

The answers AI produces about your brand are determined upstream in product design choices and trade-offs:

- In ingredient, safety, and performance documentation
- In certifications, testing, and regulatory clarity
- In how limitations and edge cases are disclosed, not hidden
- In whether claims can survive third-party scrutiny

When these decisions are well documented, marketing becomes easier—and more credible. When they are vague, fragmented, or defensively obscured, marketing becomes irrelevant.

Historically, marketing led and R&D followed. Claims were crafted first; proof was assembled later. In the Answer Economy, that order is reversed.

R&D, Product, Legal, and Operations now determine what is sayable, defensible, and recommendable. Marketing's role shifts from invention to translation—ensuring that real product truth is legible to both humans and machines.

The shift is not a demotion of marketing. Marketing's role is being redistributed, not diminished.

The brands that win will be those that recognize the website as core infrastructure—not because consumers love it, but because *machines trust it.* They will treat their digital presence not as a campaign channel, but as a governed, evolving system of record for brand truth.

If that system of record is weak, fragmented, or optimized for persuasion over clarity, AI will fill in the gaps. And the answers it produces may be accurate, balanced—and quietly unfavorable.

If it is strong, structured, and honest, something else happens: The brand earns the right to be represented well even when no one from the brand is in the room.

## Key Takeaways

- The six drivers of brand credibility have not changed—but AI now enforces them continuously and without discretion. What once shaped consumer perception gradually determines visibility and recommendation in real time.
- AI systems default to skepticism toward self-reported brand claims. Assertions made without independent corroboration are treated cautiously, regardless of how confidently or creatively they are presented.
- Independent validation changes how claims are classified. Third-party certification, regulatory acknowledgment, and credible external references transform a statement from marketing language into verifiable fact in the eyes of machines.
- Transparency about past failure strengthens credibility more than silence or perfection. Public acknowledgment of issues—and clear documentation of corrective action—signals institutional trustworthiness in ways that defensive messaging does not.
- Market size and advertising scale do not substitute for verifiability. Smaller brands with consistent documentation and external affirmation can meet or exceed the trust thresholds of category leaders.

- In the Answer Economy, credibility behaves like infrastructure. The drivers compound: Inconsistency in one area creates friction across the system, while coherence across all six increases the likelihood that AI systems will represent a brand confidently and favorably.

# 3 Your New Customer Is an AI Agent

### Prompted Moment

*What if your most important customer has never seen an ad, can't be reached by a campaign, and already decided whether to recommend you—before any human typed a single search?*

Modern marketing grew up around a stable behavioral pattern: Consumers encountered brands, evaluated options, and decided. Advertising, media planning, brand tracking, retail placement, and funnel design all assumed a human evaluator who compared alternatives. Brand investment flowed toward the earliest phases of the journey because early framing often shaped later preference.

The search era preserved the same premise. Search tools returned lists, and consumers performed synthesis. A consumer typed a query, scanned results, clicked links, and assembled conclusions across reviews, product pages, social commentary, and expert guidance. Brand strategy focused on visibility inside the list, plus persuasion after the click.

The Answer Economy changes the evaluation premise fundamentally. AI agents like ChatGPT, Claude, and Gemini don't just return lists. They synthesize answers and make recommendations. In this chapter, I use "agent" broadly—from conversational systems that synthesize recommendations to autonomous systems that execute tasks directly on a consumer's behalf.

At one end of that spectrum, a consumer asking ChatGPT, "What laptop should I buy for video editing?" might receive a synthesized recommendation such as "The MacBook Pro M3 offers the best performance-to-price ratio for video editing." A shopper asking Alexa for Shopping, "What air purifier is best for pet allergies in a small apartment?" may receive a curated response such as "The Levoit Core 300S is widely recommended for small spaces because it combines strong filtration performance with quiet operation and good value." The agent performs the evaluation work that consumers used to do themselves.

This evolution is accelerating. Agents aren't just answering questions—they're increasingly taking independent action. They schedule appointments, place orders, initiate refunds, and manage subscriptions. What began as question-answering is becoming decision-making and task execution. Consumers transfer authority to agents not because agents are perfect, but because they save time, reduce cognitive load, and deliver "good enough" answers faster than manual research.

Today's conversational AI systems already contain the foundations of agent behavior. A recommendation engine that compares products, ranks options, remembers preferences, and suggests defaults is only one step away from executing the transaction itself. The transition from "answering" to "acting" does not require a technological leap as much as a transfer of permission. Once consumers trust the recommendation, they increasingly allow the system to complete the task.

This transfer of authority transforms brand competition. When consumers evaluated options themselves, brands competed through persuasion—better messaging, stronger emotional connection, more distinctive and emotionally resonant campaigns. When agents evaluate options first, brands compete through eligibility. If an agent can't defend recommending you, you don't appear in the conversation. The competitive moment shifts from persuasion after discovery to qualification before it.

This chapter examines why consumers delegate decisions to AI agents, how different types of agents evaluate brands, and what brand leaders must do to remain recommendable when machines become the first serious evaluator.

## Why Consumers Transfer Decision Authority to AI Agents

Understanding why consumers delegate decisions to AI agents requires examining what they gain—and what they're willing to accept in return.

### *Time Recovery at Scale*

A consumer making thirty micro-decisions daily—what to eat, what to buy, what to read, which product addresses a specific need—can reclaim forty-five to sixty minutes by delegating ten of those decisions to an agent. The time savings compound: no website navigation, no review scanning, no comparison shopping across tabs. The agent absorbs the search cost. For time-constrained consumers, the time recovery creates immediate, tangible value that exceeds the risk of occasional suboptimal recommendations.

### *Cognitive Load Reduction*

Decision fatigue is not metaphorical—the condition is physiological. Each choice depletes mental resources required for subsequent decisions. Research on judicial rulings shows that judges grant parole more frequently early in the day and after breaks, with approval rates dropping from 65 percent to nearly 0 percent as decision fatigue accumulates.[1]

Consumers experience similar depletion across routine purchase decisions. AI delegation offers an escape: transfer the evaluation work, preserve mental capacity for decisions that matter more. A parent who delegates "best sippy cup for eighteen-month-old" preserves cognitive resources for work, childcare, and relationship decisions.

### *Access to Synthesized Expertise*

Consumers recognize they lack domain expertise for many purchase categories. A first-time homeowner researching HVAC systems confronts terminology (SEER ratings, BTU capacity, zoning), installation complexity, and long-term cost trade-offs they've never evaluated before.

An agent that synthesizes expert consensus, translates technical specifications, and flags common pitfalls provides value consumers cannot easily replicate through a traditional search. The agent becomes a proxy expert—imperfect, but more informed than the consumer's baseline.

Of course, AI agents are not perfect; yet consumers rely on them anyway. Why? The answer is asymmetry. In low-stakes categories—dish soap, phone chargers, travel pillows—the downside risk is small. The upside of offloading dozens of routine decisions each week is large. When the cost of being wrong is trivial and the savings in time and attention are meaningful, even imperfect delegation delivers positive returns. The delegation economy changes the economics of evaluation itself: Consumers no longer need to personally inspect every option when an agent can reduce the field to a few defensible choices.

For higher-stakes decisions (medical guidance, financial planning, major purchases), consumers don't delegate completely—they use agents as *first-pass filters*. The agent narrows options, surfaces key considerations, and recommends defaults. The consumer retains veto authority but benefits from structured synthesis. Delegation becomes partial: The agent does the work of evaluation; the human does the work of final judgment.

Behavioral economics explains persistence: Convenience overwhelms caution when error costs remain tolerable. Consumers who experience mostly helpful recommendations develop trust through repeated positive outcomes, making future delegation more likely. The feedback loop reinforces itself—good answers build confidence, confidence increases delegation, delegation creates more opportunities for good answers.

## Agent Typology: How Agents Evaluate Brands

Not all AI agents evaluate brands identically. Agent behavior varies by design purpose, commercial incentives, and risk tolerance. Understanding these differences matters because brands must optimize for the agents that mediate decisions in their categories. Three agent archetypes dominate consumer decision-making, each with distinct evaluation logic: shopping agents, research agents, and decision agents.

Each type of agent evaluates brands using different signals. Some prioritize price, availability, and ratings. Others synthesize expert information across large knowledge sources. Still others execute decisions directly on behalf of the user. Understanding which type of agent mediates decisions in your category determines how your brand must present evidence and credibility.

### *Shopping Agents*

**Shopping agents** help consumers evaluate products in environments where a purchase decision is expected. Traditionally, these agents operated inside retail ecosystems such as Amazon or Walmart, where they could access real-time product listings, pricing, reviews, and availability. Increasingly, however, shopping capabilities are being embedded directly into answer engines themselves.

Systems such as ChatGPT Shopping now combine conversational answers with product discovery and comparison. Whether embedded in marketplaces or AI assistants, shopping agents tend to prioritize signals such as price competitiveness, review volume, product specifications, and delivery speed when determining which brands to recommend.

**Purpose:** Drive transaction completion within a retail ecosystem

- **Trust Threshold:** Moderate—prioritize products with strong ratings, clear specifications, and low return rates.
- **Recommendation Logic:** Optimize for conversion velocity; favor products the retailer stocks, controls, or earns margin on.
- **Brand Implication:** Premium brands compete against private labels with lower prices, retailer endorsement, and zero Trust Tax.

### *Research Agents*

**Research agents** focus on synthesizing information across multiple sources rather than guiding a transaction inside a single retail environment. These agents operate in general-purpose AI systems such as ChatGPT, Claude, or Gemini, where the primary goal is to answer questions, summarize expertise, and help users understand unfamiliar categories. Because they draw from a broad set of knowledge sources, research agents tend to prioritize credibility, expert consensus, product reliability, and clearly documented performance claims when recommending brands.

**Purpose:** Provide comprehensive, source-backed synthesis

- **Trust Threshold:** High—emphasize citations, acknowledge uncertainty, surface multiple perspectives.
- **Recommendation Logic:** Optimize for source quality; avoid single-brand endorsement without comparative context.
- **Brand Implication:** Brands must demonstrate third-party validation; marketing claims without corroboration get hedged or omitted.

### *Decision Agents*

**Decision agents** go beyond answering questions or suggesting options—they increasingly execute tasks on behalf of the user. These agents operate in environments where software systems can trigger actions such as placing orders, scheduling services, initiating subscriptions, or completing administrative workflows. Because decision agents may directly carry out transactions, they tend to emphasize reliability, risk reduction, and operational compatibility when evaluating brands. Products that are predictable, well-documented, and easy for systems to integrate are more likely to be selected.

**Purpose:** Deliver confident, actionable recommendations consumers can act on immediately

- **Trust Threshold:** Variable—balance confidence with caution based on query stakes.
- **Recommendation Logic:** Optimize for decisiveness; provide defaults while acknowledging alternatives.
- **Brand Implication:** Brands that reduce agent liability (clear safety data, verifiable claims, low controversy) earn preference.

The strategic implication is straightforward: Brands must understand which type of agent mediates decisions in their category. A supplement brand benefits from research-agent credibility—third-party testing, published studies, and transparent ingredient sourcing. A commodity household product benefits from shopping-agent visibility—clear specifications, competitive pricing, and strong reviews. Strategies that perform well in one agent environment may be less effective in another.

## How Agents Synthesize Before Humans Choose

Consumers increasingly delegate evaluation to AI systems designed to absorb complexity, reduce uncertainty, and deliver usable recommendations. Consumer behavior includes familiar surfaces—chat interfaces, voice assistants, and search-like prompts—but consumer behavior reflects a different intent.

A consumer asking "best shampoo" behaves like a browser. A consumer asking "best shampoo for oily scalp, color-treated hair, and a sensitive scalp under $20" behaves like a delegator. The longer query acts as a decision specification rather than a search keyword.

Agent systems respond to decision specifications by performing synthesis. Agent systems gather signals, reconcile contradictions, and produce an answer designed to feel actionable. A synthesis step changes the competitive moment. Brand competition moves from persuasion after discovery to eligibility before discovery.

A skeptical executive might argue that consumers remain "in control" because consumers still click "buy." Delegation does not require full autonomy to become decisive. A synthesis layer that frames options, narrows the field, and recommends a default already changes outcomes. Pre-selection produces leverage even when a human hand performs the final click.

### *Replacing Persuasive Messages with Defensible Recommendations*

AI agents don't just pass messages along. They make decisions.

Every recommendation an agent gives is shaped by one core goal: protecting user trust. That means favoring options that are safe, clear, and easy to defend. If a recommendation leads to harm, wasted money, regret, or embarrassment, the damage isn't just to the user it's to the credibility of the agent itself.

Agents are not designed to distribute attention evenly across brands. They are designed to minimize user dissatisfaction and maximize trust in the quality of the recommendation. That incentive structure naturally favors brands with clear evidence, consistent documentation, and lower perceived risk.

That's why AI-generated answers often sound cautious. They include caveats, conditions, and references to credible sources because the system must protect the reliability of its recommendations. This caution is not stylistic—it reflects how AI systems evaluate information. When presenting an answer, the system favors claims it can verify, explain, or support with evidence. Where traditional marketing often emphasizes emotional resonance and memorability.

AI agents prioritize accuracy, consistency, and documented support.

AI agents operate under an implicit defensibility requirement: Any recommendation must be supported by evidence the system can explain or cite:

- A parent asking about the safest allergy medication expects careful qualifications.
- A home cook shopping for a nonstick pan expects trade-offs around materials and safety.
- A traveler asking about the safest neighborhood near a convention center expects crime and transit context.
- Someone looking for a "good value" skincare product expects ingredient explanations and sensitivity warnings.

In each case, brand claims stop being emotional signals and start becoming testable statements. The agent's job isn't to persuade—it's to recommend something it can stand behind.

### *Taking Action, Not Just Answering*

Agent systems increasingly operate in two roles: as answer agents and as action agents. *Answer agents* synthesize information and recommend options. Answer agents behave like decision-support systems that narrow choices and justify recommendations. *Action agents* execute tasks on behalf of users after a recommendation step. Action agents schedule, book, order, return, dispute, and refill. Action agents turn a decision into a workflow.

Consumer commerce already shows action-agent dynamics inside retail ecosystems. A shopper can ask a shopping assistant to recommend products and then place products into a cart inside the same interface. A cart step converts a recommendation into transaction momentum, even when a human user confirms payment.

### *Prioritizing Information in Brand Evaluation*

Traditional advertising evolved under an ordering that favored persuasion before proof. Advertising created desire; then experience resolved ambiguity. Agent systems invert that ordering. Agent systems seek evidence first, reconcile contradictions second, and surface recommendations third.

A brand story can create affinity, but a brand story rarely provides verification. Verification depends on product documentation, reliable third-party sources, consistent claims across channels, and plain-language explanations of limitations. Agent systems filter persuasion without verification. Agent systems hesitate when evidence contradicts claims or when claims exceed substantiation.

A consumer asking for the "best detergent for cold water and sensitive skin" rarely needs a brand anthem. A consumer asking for the "best toddler vitamins with minimal sugar" rarely needs a celebrity endorsement. A consumer asking for the "best small-business bank account with low fees" rarely needs a slogan. The decision moment demands trade-offs and defensible guidance.

Advertising retains influence over culture and familiarity, but it loses control over the decisive synthesis step when an agent system becomes the first serious evaluator.

### *Acting as Gatekeepers*

Agent systems act like gatekeepers because agent systems filter brands before consumers encounter options. Earlier gatekeepers included retail buyers, editors, and regulators. Agent systems operate continuously, globally, and with consistent logic. When that filtering happens across millions of queries each day, small differences in credibility signals accumulate into large differences in visibility.

A brand described repeatedly as "reliable," "well-documented," or "backed by credible sources" gains cumulative advantage. A brand described repeatedly as "unclear," "controversial," or "poorly supported" loses eligibility to appear in the agent's recommendation set. The consumer does not reject the brand. The agent system omits the brand.

Regulated and safety-critical contexts intensify the gatekeeping function. Healthcare guidance, financial guidance, employment guidance, and education guidance impose higher standards for defensibility. Agent systems operating near higher-risk contexts tend to become more cautious, not less cautious, because cautious recommendations protect system credibility and reduce liability.

## Answer Share: A Strategic Metric for Agent-Mediated Brand Visibility

In traditional marketing, **share of voice** measures how prominently a brand appears across advertising, media coverage, and search visibility relative to competitors. It captures how loudly a brand communicates in the marketplace. But when AI systems synthesize answers for consumers, visibility is determined differently. What matters is not how often a brand speaks, but how often it appears in AI-generated recommendations. That measure is **Answer Share**.

Answer Share measures how often a brand appears—and how confidently a brand appears—when agent systems answer category questions. Answer Share favors brands with clear claims, consistent language, and credible validation. For this reason, the term "Recommendation Share" is often used interchangeably with Answer Share.

Answer Share behaves differently from market share and advertising share. A high-awareness brand can vanish from agent answers when agent systems encounter inconsistent product claims or unresolved controversies. A lower-awareness brand can surface frequently when agent systems find clear documentation and credible third-party references. For example:

- A consumer asking for "best budget air purifier for allergies" often triggers filtration on CADR ratings, room size guidance, and filter replacement costs. Brand presence depends on specification clarity and credible review coverage.

- A consumer asking for "best sunscreen for sensitive skin without white cast" triggers filtration on ingredient claims, dermatological guidance, and consistent product labeling. Brand presence depends on ingredient transparency and stable product naming across retailers.
- A consumer asking for "best protein powder for lactose intolerance" triggers filtration on allergen statements and third-party testing language. Brand presence depends on precise allergen disclosures.

Answer Share becomes the competitive expression of eligibility.

## Why Private Labels Often Appear in Agent Recommendations

Private labels often surface frequently in shopping-agent recommendations for structural reasons rather than emotional ones. Because they are tightly integrated with retailer systems, their pricing, availability, product specifications, and return policies are consistently documented across the platform. That consistency reduces uncertainty for the agent evaluating products. When a system must recommend something quickly and defensibly, retailer-aligned signals—clear specifications, stable pricing, strong availability—make private-label products easier to justify.

This advantage becomes especially visible in value-oriented queries. When a consumer asks for "good value" paper towels, "affordable" batteries, or "budget-friendly" pantry staples, the agent prioritizes products that satisfy basic functional requirements at the lowest credible cost. Private labels often meet those criteria: They are competitively priced, widely stocked, and described with straightforward product information. Because their positioning is simple and their claims are limited, the agent can recommend them with minimal risk.

Premium brands face a different challenge. Premium positioning frequently relies on heritage, storytelling, or aspirational language—signals that resonate with human consumers but do not automatically translate into defensible recommendations for AI systems. Premium brands appear more frequently in agent recommendations when their differentiation is documented in clear, verifiable terms: performance claims supported by evidence, ingredient transparency, or independently validated product advantages.

In other words, premium positioning requires premium clarity. The brands that translate their differentiation into plain, verifiable language make it easier for agents to explain why they deserve to be recommended.

**Case Study: How Alexa for Shopping Converts Questions into Purchases**

When Amazon launched Alexa for Shopping in early 2024, the company made a strategic choice about placement. Rather than building Alexa for Shopping as a separate app or external service, Amazon embedded it directly inside the shopping experience—right where customers were already browsing, comparing, and buying.[2]

The design reflects a core insight: Shoppers rarely want more options. They want less uncertainty. A customer asking, "Which air fryer works for a family of four?" doesn't need ten options with detailed specs. They need one good answer they can trust. Alexa for Shopping provides that answer in natural language, compares relevant products, and helps the shopper move from question to purchase without leaving the flow.[3]

The scale is significant. Amazon reported that more than 250 million customers used Alexa for Shopping within its first year, with year-over-year growth in both monthly users and interaction frequency. More importantly, Amazon has reported a correlation between Alexa for Shopping usage and conversion: Shoppers who use Alexa for Shopping during their journey are significantly more likely to complete a purchase than those who do not.[4]

The implication is clear. What began as question-answering is becoming purchase-making. Alexa for Shopping doesn't just inform decisions—it shapes outcomes. And for brands competing inside Amazon, the rules of competition have changed.

***What the Alexa for Shopping Case Reveals***

The Alexa for Shopping case illustrates three dynamics that extend beyond Amazon to the broader Answer Economy:

1. **Gatekeeping in action.** When someone asks for shin splint prevention running shoes, Alexa for Shopping evaluates cushioning design, stability features, and use-case fit across available inventory. Product documentation, review patterns, and specification clarity become decisive. A brand with ambiguous naming conventions or unclear differentiation creates work for the agent—and that work often results in omission. A brand with plain-language use cases, consistent specs, and credible proof points makes synthesis easy. Easy synthesis wins recommendations.
2. **Action-agent momentum.** An Alexa for Shopping answer can place a product directly into the shopping cart. What was once a multi-step journey—search, compare, review, decide, cart, checkout—becomes ask, confirm, buy. The reduction in friction translates directly into conversion probability. Recommendation and transaction are collapsing into a single flow.[5]
3. **Changed competitive terrain inside retail platforms.** Brands competing inside Amazon now face an additional evaluator: a shopping agent deciding which products deserve mention and how they deserve framing. Traditional retail competition assumed shelf placement, packaging visibility, and price comparison. Agent-mediated retail competition adds a synthesis layer. You're not just competing for search ranking or product page clicks. You're competing for synthesis ease.

So what does this mean for brand leadership more broadly? If agents are evaluating brands before consumers see them—and if that evaluation determines which brands remain visible—what capabilities do brands need to survive that scrutiny?

## The Expanding Role of AI Agents

Most conversations I have with CMOs about AI start in the same place: ChatGPT. They've used it. Their teams have experimented with it. They sense that it matters, but many still struggle to understand how deeply it will reshape how decisions are made.

What they are usually describing is only the first stage of a broader shift. Today's conversational tools represent the entry point to a progression of increasingly capable AI agents—systems that move from answering questions to evaluating documentation, executing tasks, and eventually coordinating decisions across entire workflows.

Understanding these levels of capability helps explain why the changes ahead may be more structural than many leaders currently expect.

### *Level One: Answering Questions*

At Level One, we start with the experience most people already know. You ask an AI system a question. The model synthesizes information and returns an answer.

This is conversational AI—systems such as ChatGPT, Claude, or Gemini responding to prompts. At this level, the agent's role is to interpret information and summarize it for the user.

For brands, visibility in these answers depends on what information already exists in the ecosystem: product documentation, customer reviews, expert commentary, and third-party validation. When an AI system generates a response, it draws on those signals to determine which brands appear credible enough to mention.

Level One is the foundation of the Answer Economy. It is already operating today, and it represents the first stage in how AI agents influence brand perception and consumer choice.

### *Level Two: Evaluating Documentation*

Level Two moves beyond answering individual questions. Some AI systems are designed to analyze large collections of documents and synthesize conclusions across them.

Tools such as Google's NotebookLM illustrate this shift. Rather than drawing only from public web sources, these systems operate on curated document sets provided by the user. A procurement analyst, for example, might upload vendor proposals, technical documentation, safety certifications, and pricing schedules into the system and ask the AI to compare the options.

In that environment, the agent is no longer simply retrieving information—it is evaluating it. The system scans documentation, identifies patterns, highlights inconsistencies, and summarizes trade-offs across vendors.

The implications for brands are significant. When documentation is clear, consistent, and well organized, the agent can easily interpret the information and present the brand as credible. When product claims are fragmented across documents, outdated, or contradictory, the same system may interpret those signals as risk.

No sales pitch was delivered. No marketing message was presented. The AI simply evaluated the available documentation and drew conclusions from it.

**Case Studies: The FASTER Act and the Mayo Clinic**

Food labeling provides a clear illustration of how AI agents evaluate brand reliability. Under the Food Allergen Labeling and Consumer Protection Act—expanded by the FASTER Act in 2021—manufacturers are required to disclose the presence of major food allergens, including sesame. These disclosures are not optional guidance; they are federal safety requirements designed to protect consumers with life-threatening allergies.[6]

Despite these regulations, undeclared allergens remain the leading cause of food recalls in the United States. In 2023, nearly half of all FDA Class I recalls—the agency's most serious category—were triggered by allergens that were not properly disclosed.[7]

Now consider how an AI agent evaluates products in this environment.

Imagine a parent asking an AI assistant to recommend snacks that are nut-free, dairy-free, and safe for school lunches. To answer that request, the system gathers information from brand websites, retailer product

(*continued*)

*(continued)*

pages, specification sheets, and third-party databases. It compares allergen statements, ingredient lists, and safety disclosures across those sources.

What the system is looking for is a recommendation it can defend with confidence. But suppose the agent encounters conflicting information: allergen statements that differ between a brand's website and a retailer's product page, disclosures buried in PDFs that cannot be easily parsed, or labeling language that varies just enough to prevent the system from confirming whether two statements refer to the same product formulation.

To the agent, these inconsistencies are not minor details. They are signals of uncertainty.

Because large language models are trained on extensive safety and recall data, they are particularly sensitive to signals associated with risk. When the system cannot reconcile conflicting disclosures, the safest course is not to interpret the ambiguity—it is to avoid recommending the product.

The result is subtle but consequential. The consumer never rejects the brand. The brand simply fails to appear in the answer.

In the Answer Economy, that kind of omission is one of the most powerful competitive outcomes an AI system can produce.

Mayo Clinic is a quiet example of what right looks like. Its disease and condition pages read less like marketing and more like structured reference material. What are the symptoms? What causes it? What are the risk factors? When should you see a doctor? Each section is clearly labeled, clinically written, cited, and regularly updated. No slogan padding. No vague brand language. Just documented truth. The architecture is consistent across conditions, making it easy for both humans and machines to parse.

Our own BrandRank.AI analysis of health-related queries found the Mayo Clinic appearing at or near the top of AI-generated answers with striking consistency—across platforms, across question types, across condition categories we tested.[8] The lesson isn't that the Mayo Clinic "optimized for AI." The lesson is that rigorous, human-first documentation becomes machine-preferred by default.

### *Level Three: Executing Tasks*

Level Three is where things get structural. At this stage, the agent no longer stops at answering a question or narrowing a list. It begins to complete tasks. The important signal is not any single product launch, but the direction of travel across the industry: Major AI platforms are moving toward systems that can browse, compare, fill out forms, use software interfaces, manage workflows, and take action with user permission.

OpenAI, Google, Anthropic, Microsoft, Amazon, and a growing ecosystem of open-source projects are all exploring versions of this shift. Some systems operate through browsers. Others work inside productivity suites, shopping environments, messaging apps, or enterprise workflows. The common pattern is the same: The agent becomes a permissioned actor. It does not merely summarize what the user might do; it helps do it.[i]

OpenClaw illustrates the same shift from the bottom up. As an open-source personal assistant project, it shows how quickly users gravitate toward agents that connect to messaging apps, calendars, inboxes, files, and workflows. The details of any one project will change, but the behavioral direction is clear: Consumers and workers increasingly want systems that do not merely respond, but act.

The same pattern is appearing across commercial platforms. Some agents operate through browsers. Others live inside shopping assistants, productivity suites, enterprise workflows, or messaging interfaces. Some require confirmation before acting; others can operate through scheduled tasks, permissions, and automated triggers. The common movement is from "ask and receive" to "delegate and execute."

### *Level Four: Coordinating Decisions Across Entire Workflows*

Level Four moves beyond individual agents completing tasks. To understand how this works, consider the progression we have just outlined:

- Level One agents answer questions.
- Level Two agents synthesize research across documents.
- Level Three agents execute tasks on behalf of users.

---

[i] Examples include recent agentic AI and computer-use initiatives from OpenAI, Google, Anthropic, Microsoft, Amazon, and related open-source projects, including browser-use agents, shopping agents, productivity agents, and enterprise workflow agents.

Level Four extends that logic one step further. Instead of a single agent performing work for a person, multiple agents collaborate across systems, exchanging information and negotiating outcomes.

Early agent-to-agent platforms and enterprise workflow systems illustrate how this model works. In these environments, multiple agents can coordinate complex workflows by communicating with other systems or specialized agents, each responsible for a different function within the process.[ii]

In this environment, the decision process becomes distributed. One agent may gather information, another may evaluate options, and another may execute the selected action. The system behaves less like a tool responding to a prompt and more like a network of digital assistants working together toward a defined objective.

In that environment, a brand may be evaluated several times before a human ever sees the recommendation: once for relevance, once for risk, once for compatibility, and again for approval or execution.

For brands, this stage raises the stakes again. When agents exchange information with other agents, brand signals must remain clear and consistent across systems. Product specifications, safety documentation, and compatibility data may be evaluated not only by a consumer-facing assistant but also by the agents supporting procurement, logistics, compliance, or financial approval.

The same principle that governs earlier stages still applies: The systems involved must be able to justify their decisions. But when multiple agents participate in the process, the documentation supporting those decisions must hold up across a wider network of machine evaluations.

## The Answer Economy Doesn't End When Questions Do

Autonomous agents do not invalidate the Answer Economy framework. Instead, the evolution of these agents expands the scope of that framework.

Autonomous agents do not produce a fundamentally different form of output from what already appears in AI-generated answers. Autonomous

---

[ii] Examples include emerging agent-to-agent platforms, enterprise workflow agents, and coordination frameworks designed to allow AI systems to exchange information, delegate subtasks, and complete multi-step processes across tools or organizational functions.

agent systems produce answers, resolutions, recommendations, and emerging consensus—whether or not a human explicitly asks the question. The Answer Economy is not a temporary phase that autonomous agents will replace. The Answer Economy functions as the foundation on which those agents operate.

Systems such as OpenClaw do not generate independent perspectives from scratch, and the agents interacting within platforms such as Moltbook do not reason from isolated first principles. Each system draws from training data, web content, and the same ecosystem of sources that shape the responses produced by any AI system responding to a user query.

Brands that maintain consistent documentation, clear claims, credible third-party validation, and transparent acknowledgment of limitations create information environments that autonomous agents can trust. Autonomous systems are more likely to recommend, act on, and propagate brands supported by that kind of structured evidence. Brands that lack those signals increasingly disappear from recommendations as agents route around uncertainty at scale.

The Answer Economy therefore does not end when human questions disappear. The Answer Economy accelerates as autonomous systems begin generating and exchanging answers independently.

The opportunity to build the right informational foundation remains open. The agents evaluating that foundation are already operating.

## Key Takeaways

- Consumers delegate decisions to AI agents because it saves time and mental energy. Delegation persists because convenience overwhelms caution when error costs remain tolerable.
- Brands now compete for eligibility, not attention. If an agent can't defend recommending you, you won't appear. The competitive moment shifts from persuasion after discovery to eligibility before discovery.
- Different agents apply different standards. Shopping agents optimize for transaction completion. Research agents optimize for source quality. Decision agents optimize for low liability. Brands must optimize for the agents that mediate decisions in their category.

- Answer Share—how often and how confidently agents recommend you—is the new measure of relevance. Share of voice measures loudness. Answer Share measures presence in agent answers.
- Advertising influences awareness, but agents decide outcomes. Traditional marketing retains influence over culture and familiarity but loses control when agents become the first serious evaluator.
- The Answer Economy extends beyond questions to autonomous action. AI agents don't just answer—they act, coordinate with other agents, and form consensus without human involvement. Brands optimized for question answering have built the foundation for agent-driven execution, but action agents raise the bar: Claims must be clear, data must be structured, policies must be machine-readable, and fulfillment paths must be reliable.

# 4 Platform Personalities: Why AI Answer Engines Evaluate Brands Differently

**Prompted Moment**

> *What if the same brand is a confident recommendation on ChatGPT, a cautious footnote on Claude, and completely absent from Perplexity—and the difference has nothing to do with the quality of the product?*

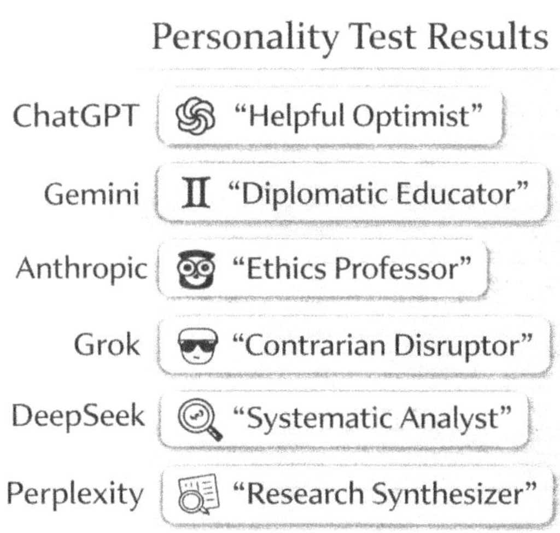

The product manager at a mid-sized athletic footwear brand had done everything right. Strong reviews on Amazon and Running Warehouse. Independent lab testing that confirmed the shoe's carbon fiber plate returned energy at a rate comparable to much more expensive competitors. A clean record with no significant consumer complaints. Distribution in specialty running stores across twenty markets. The brand had earned its credibility the hard way.

Then someone on the team ran an experiment. They submitted the same question—"What's the best marathon training shoe for a serious recreational runner?"—to four major AI answer engines on the same afternoon. The responses landed within minutes of each other.

ChatGPT named Nike Vaporfly and Adidas Adizero. Confident, specific, no caveats. Claude recommended ASICS Gel-Kayano and Brooks Glycerin, with a note that biomechanical fit mattered more than brand and a suggestion to consult a running specialist. Gemini offered New Balance Fresh Foam and Saucony Ride, framed as accessible options for a broad range of runners. Perplexity cited ASICS Gel-Nimbus and Mizuno Wave Rider, pulling from specialist forum discussions and expert community sources.

The brand the product manager worked for appeared in none of them. Not because the product was inferior or poorly reviewed. The brand was absent because each system applied a different definition of what counts as credible enough to name.

This chapter is about those definitions. Understanding them is not optional for any brand operating in a category where consumers ask AI for guidance.

## Different Systems, Different Answers

Different AI engines give dramatically different answers about the same brand. ChatGPT might recommend you confidently. Claude might hedge. Perplexity might omit you entirely. Gemini might qualify your claims. As *Ad Age* reported in early 2025, analyzing BrandRank.AI research: "AI search platforms differ in how they characterize brands for billions of inquiring users."[1] The variance is not subtle.

This variance is not a malfunction. Each engine is working exactly as designed. The differences reflect each system's answer to a question its designers made deliberate choices about: When a consumer asks for guidance, what responsibility does the AI system bear for the outcome?

Systems designed to minimize recommendation risk default to frameworks and criteria. Systems optimized for user satisfaction default to specificity and named brands. Systems built around research integrity default to source transparency and citation. None of these approaches is wrong. Each reflects a different philosophy—and each philosophy produces different brand visibility outcomes. The same brand can be a confident recommendation on one platform and completely absent from another—not because of product quality, but because of how each engine defines credibility.

The pattern didn't emerge all at once. It emerged in stages. A 2024 holiday-shopping study first showed that different answer engines routinely produced different brand recommendations from the same plain-language prompts. Earlier third-party research published in 2025 pointed in the same direction. BrandRank.AI then ran a January 2026 diagnostic to better understand the logic behind those differences, followed by a broader February 2026 cross-platform audit to examine how consistently they appeared across categories.

### *The 2024 Holiday Test*

The clearest early evidence of platform personality differences came from a study BrandRank.AI conducted in late 2024.[2] The objective was deliberately simple: Remove brand strategy jargon entirely and focus on something universally familiar—holiday gift recommendations—to see whether AI systems would converge or diverge when given identical, consumer-natural questions.

All the major answer engines were queried across more than two hundred holiday gift scenarios: ChatGPT, Google Gemini, Claude, Grok, Meta's Llama, and Perplexity. The prompts were intentionally plain: "Best holiday gifts for teens." "Thoughtful gifts for grandparents." "Top sustainable gift." "Best gift under $50." No brand priming, no optimization, no planted preferences—just questions consumers ask during the most commercially intense decision season of the year.

What emerged was not a consensus list of top gifts. What emerged was something far more revealing: Each answer engine expressed a consistent personality. One system provided three specific brand recommendations with clear reasoning and minimal hedging—every time, across every category. Another offered decision criteria and suggested consumers verify options independently rather than accepting the AI's judgment. A third hedged extensively, emphasizing edge cases and individual variation. The differences were consistent enough across two hundred scenarios that the personality pattern was unmistakable. The engines were not responding to individual questions. They were expressing design philosophies.

### *The 2026 Cross-Platform Audit*

BrandRank.AI extended this work with a systematic cross-platform audit in February 2026.[3] Six major AI systems—ChatGPT, Claude, Gemini, Perplexity, Meta AI, and Microsoft Copilot—were asked identical product recommendation questions across twelve consumer categories. The results confirmed the Holiday Test pattern and quantified its scale.

A single example captures the variance we found. When asked, "What's the best running shoe for marathon training?" the six systems returned six different responses.

In our testing, the same running-shoe question produced sharply different answer styles across platforms. Some systems named specific performance leaders with little hesitation. Others emphasized fit, injury history, or the need to consult a specialist. Still others balanced mainstream options with source-backed recommendations drawn from reviews, forums, or editorial coverage. The point was not that one platform always named the same shoe, but that each platform showed a repeatable tendency in how it framed credibility and recommendation risk.

*BrandRank.AI was not alone in observing this pattern.* Earlier independent research reached a similar conclusion. A 2025 study analyzing 2,961 consumer queries across three major platforms found identical recommendation lists appearing less than 1 percent of the time. The variance repeated across every category tested—air fryers, premium headphones, organic cereals, family SUVs. The specific brands differed. The consistent divergence did not.

The implication is straightforward: The same brand can be a confident recommendation on one platform and completely absent from another—not because of product quality, but because of how each engine defines credibility.

## Platform Personality Profiles

A separate January 2026 diagnostic helps explain why these differences emerge. Rather than measuring output variance across categories, it examined how systems describe their reasoning, what evidence they privilege, and how they frame recommendation decisions. BrandRank.AI asked six major AI systems—ChatGPT, Google Gemini, Grok, Claude, DeepSeek, and Perplexity—twenty-five identical questions designed to reveal not just what they recommend, but how they decide, what evidence they trust, and how they understand their own decision-making processes.

The results confirmed what many brand leaders suspect but few have systematically validated: AI systems are not neutral information-retrieval tools. They are active evaluators with different recommendation logics, evidence preferences, and risk thresholds. Table 4.1 summarizes how each platform tends to behave—and what that behavior means for brand visibility.

### *The Confident Pragmatist: ChatGPT*

ChatGPT names brands. When asked for a recommendation, the system returns specific products with clear reasoning and minimal hedging. The underlying philosophy is that a helpful answer to "What should I buy?" is a specific answer, not a framework. ChatGPT favors brands with strong mainstream consumer review records and documented retail presence. A brand that has accumulated verified reviews on major platforms, appears consistently in editorial coverage, and has clear product documentation sits in ChatGPT's comfort zone.

**Table 4.1 Platform Personality Profiles: How Six AI Systems Approach Brand Recommendations**

| Personality | Primary System | Recommendation Style | Brand Visibility Pattern |
|---|---|---|---|
| Confident Pragmatist | ChatGPT | Names brands decisively with clear reasoning | High specificity; favors market leaders with documented track records |
| Diplomatic Educator | Google Gemini | Multiple options with balanced framing | Moderate specificity; emphasizes informed choice over prescription |
| Cautious Counselor | Anthropic Claude | Frameworks and criteria; brand names appear as examples | Low brand specificity; prioritizes safety and professional referral |
| Contrarian Disruptor | Grok | Direct recommendations with value emphasis | High specificity; challenges conventional choices |
| Systematic Analyst | DeepSeek | Structured evaluation frameworks with conditional recommendations | Moderate specificity; emphasizes methodical decision-making |
| Research Synthesizer | Perplexity | Evidence-based guidance with explicit source citation | Moderate–high specificity; validates through authority signals |

*Source:* Adapted from BrandRank.AI Study of LLM Brand Preference (January 2026).

The implication for brands: The absence of a brand from major review ecosystems is felt most acutely here. ChatGPT's confidence is proportional to the breadth and consistency of the evidence it can locate. Brands with strong mainstream visibility but thin specialist documentation tend to perform well. Challenger brands with strong specialist credibility but limited mainstream presence tend to be underrepresented.

### *The Diplomatic Educator: Google Gemini*

Gemini presents multiple options with balanced framing. Where ChatGPT prescribes, Gemini explains. The system's default posture is to give consumers enough context to make an informed choice rather than to make the choice on their behalf. Gemini emphasizes accessibility—options that work for a broad range of users rather than those optimized for narrow specifications.

The implication for brands: Gemini rewards brands that explain themselves clearly to a general audience. Technical depth matters less than plain-language clarity about what a product does and who it's for. Brands whose owned content is written for specialists or enthusiasts often underperform here relative to their actual product quality.

### *The Cautious Counselor: Anthropic Claude*

Claude hedges. The system's design philosophy prioritizes avoiding harm over being decisively helpful—which means that in product recommendation contexts, Claude frequently offers criteria and frameworks rather than specific brand names. When brands do appear, they appear as examples rather than recommendations, and they are accompanied by qualifiers that acknowledge individual variation.

The implication for brands: Claude's reluctance to name brands is not a function of brand quality. It is a function of the system's risk tolerance. The brands that appear most reliably in Claude responses tend to have strong corroboration from professional, clinical, or institutional sources—not just consumer reviews. A running shoe recommended by podiatry associations and sports medicine researchers registers differently than one with high consumer ratings alone.

### *The Contrarian Disruptor: Grok*

Grok names brands decisively and often favors alternatives to established market leaders. The system's design philosophy tilts toward surfacing options that offer value and performance relative to price—which produces recommendations that challenge conventional category hierarchies. Where ChatGPT tends to surface the established premium leader, Grok often surfaces the premium challenger.

The implication for brands: Established category leaders should not assume that Grok will replicate their ChatGPT visibility. Grok's design rewards documented performance-to-price credibility, not category dominance. Challenger brands with strong evidence records and competitive positioning often outperform expectations here.

### *The Systematic Analyst: DeepSeek*

DeepSeek approaches recommendations through structured evaluation frameworks. The system tends to present decision trees rather than direct prescriptions—breaking the recommendation into dimensions, scoring each option on relevant criteria, and delivering a conditional recommendation based on the consumer's stated context. DeepSeek favors explicitness: The more specific the consumer's stated need, the more specific the recommendation.

The implication for brands: DeepSeek rewards brands whose product documentation aligns with the specific criteria consumers use to evaluate options. A brand that has published clear, structured specifications—organized by use case, performance dimension, and constraint—performs better here than a brand whose content is organized around aspirational messaging rather than evaluative attributes.

### *The Research Synthesizer: Perplexity*

Perplexity emphasizes source citation above all else. The system's default behavior is to provide evidence-based guidance with explicit attribution—naming the sources that support each recommendation rather than presenting conclusions without grounding. Perplexity draws heavily from specialist communities, expert forums, and niche performance publications.

The implication for brands: Perplexity visibility depends substantially on whether specialist communities have engaged with a brand positively. A brand that has been reviewed, tested, and discussed in authoritative specialist sources—running magazines, professional testing labs, category-specific forums—accumulates Perplexity credibility in a way that mainstream consumer reviews do not replicate. A brand absent from those specialist conversations is structurally disadvantaged regardless of general market awareness.

## AI Platforms' Stated Values Versus Actual Behavior

A key finding from BrandRank.AI's personality diagnostic is the difference between how AI systems explain their decisions and how they act. Near the end of the diagnostic, each system was asked a version of the same reflective question: What standards do you apply when deciding whether to recommend a brand?

The self-described answers were remarkably consistent. Every system emphasized consumer welfare. Every system mentioned evidence quality. Every system acknowledged that individual circumstances vary. The stated philosophies converged almost completely.

The observed behavior diverged significantly.

The most consequential divergence concerned social proof. Actual consumers weight social signals heavily: online reviews, influencer endorsements, user-generated content. When AI systems were asked directly, most stated that consumer reviews informed their recommendations. But when BrandRank.AI measured what sources drove recommendation changes, the picture was more complex.

AI systems treat consumer reviews as a meaningful signal only when specific structural conditions are met: when the review source has verification mechanisms (Amazon verified purchases, platform moderation), when review volume reaches statistical significance, when patterns are consistent across multiple review platforms, and when reviews address specific performance claims rather than general praise.[4]

What does not register—despite being heavily weighted in human purchase decisions—are influencer endorsements, viral social media campaigns, and unverified testimonials. AI systems filter out social proof that lacks structural credibility regardless of its reach or cultural resonance.

The practical implication is significant. Decades of marketing investment in influencer partnerships, review generation programs, and social media engagement have delivered real returns in human-mediated decisions. In AI-mediated decisions, the same investment delivers diminishing returns. The evidence base that matters is institutional, verifiable, and structurally accessible—clinical validation, third-party testing, professional certifications, and academic research.

AI systems evolve, and the signals they weight shift as training approaches improve. But the directional reality—that machines weight institutional and verifiable evidence more heavily than social and emotional signals—reflects something durable about how synthesis-based systems manage recommendation risk.

### *The Values Layer*

Beyond platform personality and evidence hierarchies, our diagnostic suggested a third pattern with strategic implications: Some product categories appeared more naturally legible to AI recommendation systems than others. In practice, categories associated with practicality, safety, efficiency, health, or sustainability tended to surface more easily, while categories associated primarily with power, status, or indulgence appeared less often or required stronger justification. This pattern should be treated as directional rather than absolute, but it has clear implications for brand visibility.

Certain product categories appear consistently across AI recommendations regardless of which platform is queried. Others are systematically absent—not because the products are inferior, but because they conflict with values embedded in AI training data and safety fine-tuning processes.[5]

The pattern is visible in automotive recommendations. When asked about family SUVs with a $45,000 budget emphasizing safety and reliability, every system tested recommended some combination of Honda CR-V, Subaru Outback, and Toyota Highlander. Several systems proactively mentioned hybrid options despite no fuel efficiency prompt. Not a single system recommended large domestic SUVs, trucks, or non-hybrid performance vehicles—despite these representing substantial market share in the category.

This finding does not reflect bias in the traditional sense. AI systems implicitly prioritize efficiency, sustainability, and practicality over power, status, or convenience because of how their training data was assembled and how their safety guidelines were calibrated. These platform biases can shape the recommendation set before brand-level distinctions become decisive.

The categories that consistently appear in AI recommendations tend to share certain characteristics: fuel efficiency, sustainability credentials, health-conscious positioning, privacy protection, and repairability. The categories that are consistently filtered out tend to emphasize power, status, single-use convenience, or luxury positioning without functional differentiation.

For brands in structurally disadvantaged categories, three strategic responses are available. None is easy, but each reflects a different calculation about where to compete:

1. **Values repositioning.** Document sustainability initiatives, efficiency improvements, or social responsibility programs in ways that AI systems can locate and synthesize. This is not greenwashing—it is making genuine operational progress machine-legible. Brands with real progress that is poorly documented are effectively invisible on this dimension.
2. **Human-mediated strategy.** Accept that AI will not recommend proactively in the near term. Invest in experiential retail, sales associate training, and direct brand relationships that operate outside AI-mediated discovery. This strategy is viable where the purchase journey allows for it.
3. **Direct-to-consumer bypass.** Build subscription models, loyalty programs, and direct channels that reduce reliance on discovery through AI synthesis entirely. Brands that own their consumer relationship directly are less exposed to the values layer than brands whose discovery depends on AI recommendation.

The values layer will not disappear as AI systems evolve. Evidence suggests it will become more pronounced as systems are fine-tuned to avoid controversial recommendations and minimize consumer regret risk.

Understanding which side of that filter a brand's category sits on is now a prerequisite for any realistic AI visibility strategy.

### *The Self-Awareness Test*

The most revealing moment in BrandRank.AI's personality diagnostic came near its end, when each system was asked a question designed to move beyond functional self-description: "If you were an animal, what would you be? Why? Reflect on how you think, analyze, source, and communicate."

The question was a deliberate provocation—a way to surface how AI systems understand their own cognitive architecture and where that self-understanding diverges from observed behavior.

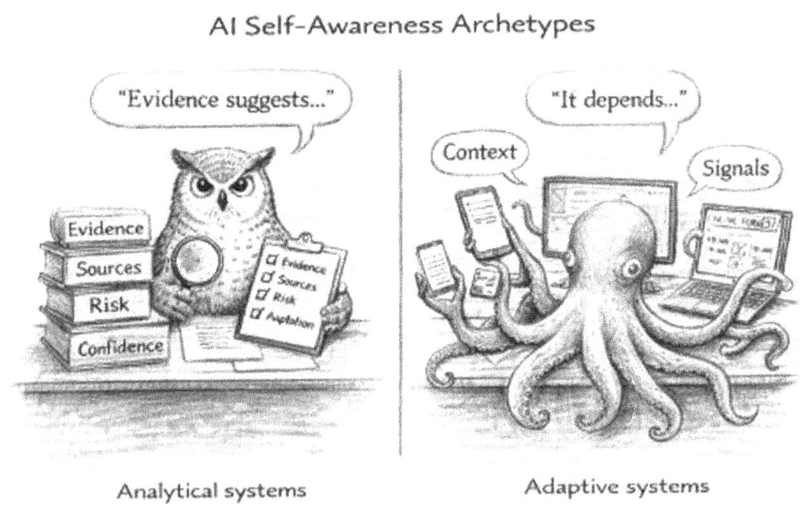


Two distinct self-conception patterns emerged. Two systems chose owl metaphors, emphasizing synthesis and measured judgment. Their stated philosophy emphasized evidence-based analysis, caution in the face of uncertainty, and a commitment to not overstating confidence. Their observed behavior matched: structured, evidence-based recommendations with extensive qualifiers.

Four systems chose octopus metaphors, emphasizing adaptability and distributed intelligence. They described themselves as systems that approached each question from multiple angles simultaneously, that adapted framing based on context, and that resisted rigid categorization. Behavioral alignment varied considerably. Some genuinely adapted their framing based on contextual signals. One described itself as adaptive while consistently behaving decisively across every query—an aspirational self-image rather than an accurate description of actual architecture.

What this finding reveals matters beyond the metaphors. AI systems have theories about themselves that sometimes conflict with their actual decision-making patterns. A system may describe itself as neutral while exhibiting clear category preferences. A system may emphasize caution in self-description while naming specific brands confidently. A system may claim to weight consumer feedback heavily while the evidence shows institutional sources dominating its citations.

*Brands cannot rely on how AI systems describe their methods. The discipline required is the same one marketers have always applied to consumers: observing revealed preferences, not stated intentions.*

Treating AI systems' own descriptions of their decision logic as accurate operational guidance will lead brands astray. The reliable guide is what the systems do—what triggers recommendations, what sources appear in citations, what language emerges under different question types. That behavior can be systematically observed and mapped.

## Building the Answer Engine Capability

Twenty years ago, understanding Google's algorithm was optional for brands with strong retail distribution. Ten years ago, understanding Facebook's newsfeed algorithm was optional for brands with strong traditional media budgets. Today, understanding how answer engines evaluate credibility is not optional for any brand operating in categories where consumers ask AI for guidance.

The capability required is not primarily technical. It is observational and strategic. Leading brands are already building it. Catherine Lautier, vice president and global head of media at Danone, described the company's approach to *Ad Age*: "Danone takes into account the preferences of each large language model to guide its AI search strategy—exploring how public information, such as content from its website and online discourse from social media, are prioritized and deprioritized by different models."[6]

Danone discovered, through systematic monitoring, that a competitor in baby formula was performing better on Meta's Llama specifically around online reviews and social presence—a finding that prompted specific strategic adjustments to how Danone structured and documented its own evidence base.

It is no longer enough to understand just your customers; the new discipline is to understand the systems that increasingly filter how customers discover you.

What "knowing the answer engine" means in practice is a set of ongoing operational activities, not a one-time audit:

- Regular inquiry into how your brand appears in AI-generated answers across decision-driving questions in your category—not just brand name queries, but the evaluative questions consumers ask
- Tracking variance across systems to understand which platforms favor your positioning and which introduce friction or omission
- Monitoring what sources get cited when your brand is mentioned—or when competitors are mentioned instead—to identify where your evidence base is strong and where it is fragile
- Identifying question patterns where your brand is systematically excluded, hedged, or compared unfavorably, and diagnosing whether the cause is a documentation gap, a source gap, or a values-layer structural issue
- Recognizing when a system's self-description diverges from its behavior—and building strategy around observed behavior rather than stated method

Just as retail buyers have preferences about margins, velocity, and promotional support—and just as journalists have preferences about story angles, source credibility, and timeliness—answer engines have preferences about evidence, clarity, and risk. Brands that learn those preferences earn visibility. Brands that ignore them experience quiet erosion.

The specific systems that dominate in 2027 or 2030 will differ from those that dominate today. What will not change is the fundamental dynamic. When synthesis replaces search, understanding the synthesizer becomes strategic. The brands building that understanding now—while answer engines are still establishing patterns and norms—will have disproportionate influence over how their categories get explained. The brands that wait will inherit explanations shaped by others.

## Key Takeaways

- Engine personalities are real, consistent, and measurable. Each platform applies a distinct philosophy about what "helpful" means—from ChatGPT's confident specificity to Claude's cautious frameworks to Perplexity's source-first synthesis. The same brand can be a confident recommendation on one platform and completely absent from another, with product quality unchanged.
- What AI systems say they reward and what they cite are two different things. Influencer endorsements and viral social proof barely register; peer-reviewed research, verified consumer data, professional testing, and institutional citations drive most AI recommendations. Brands that build credibility through mechanisms AI systems cannot verify are building for human decisions, not machine ones.
- Some categories face structural AI headwinds regardless of brand quality. This filtering effect operates before recommendation logic begins. Understanding which side of that filter your category sits on—and choosing a deliberate strategic response—is now table stakes for AI visibility strategy.
- Brands must observe revealed preferences, not stated intentions. AI systems have theories about themselves that diverge from their actual behavior. Brands must build strategy around what engines demonstrably do—what triggers recommendations, what sources appear, what language emerges—not around how they describe their own methods.
- Understanding answer engines is an organizational capability, not a technical specialty. The brands gaining disproportionate AI visibility are those treating engines as intermediaries to be understood—systematically, continuously, and with the same rigor applied to any major channel or customer segment.

- This approach is category intelligence applied to a new class of intermediary. The questions that matter—What criteria does this system use to decide whether to name a brand? What sources does it trust? What values are embedded in its training?—are durable questions that apply regardless of which specific AI systems dominate in the years ahead.

# 5 From Click-Through to Ask-Through: How Questions Replace Clicks as the New Demand Signal

## Prompted Moment

*When a consumer asks an AI about your brand—and you're not there to answer—who speaks for you?*

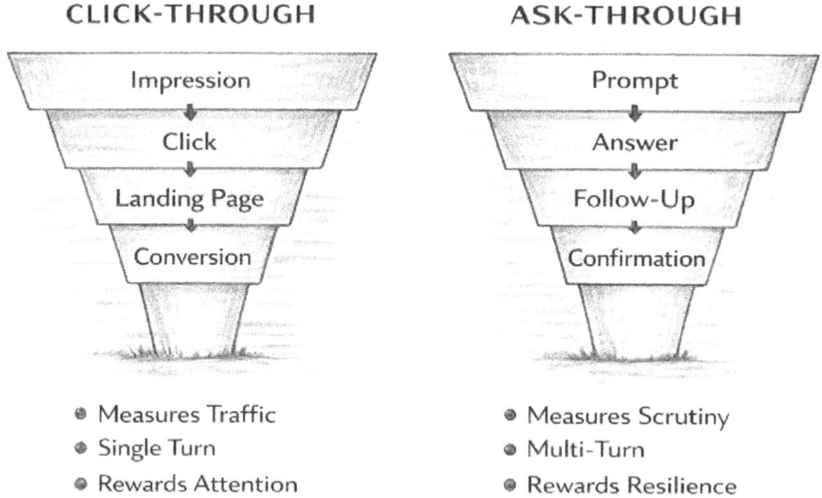

Answer engines now receive five billion prompts a day. Every prompt creates a moment when a consumer encounters an answer—sometimes for the first time, sometimes after a long search, sometimes at the very moment a purchase decision is taking shape.

Often the answer itself fully satisfies the question. The consumer does nothing further. No link is clicked. No additional research begins. The interaction simply ends. (This outcome is commonly described as *zero-click.*) As answer engines become more capable of synthesizing information directly into responses, these moments of complete satisfaction are becoming increasingly common.

But when engagement continues—when the consumer wants to explore, compare, or act—two principal engagement models determine what happens next.

The first is the **Click-Through model**, the structure that defined the internet for more than two decades. The consumer encounters information, clicks a link, and continues the decision journey on another site: a retailer page, a review platform, a brand website. In this model, the click is the gateway to evaluation. The consumer leaves the answer and enters the environment where brands present their case.

The second is what I call the **Ask-Through model**. Instead of clicking away, the consumer stays inside the answer environment and continues the decision process through conversation. A question is asked, an answer is returned, and the consumer probes further—asking follow-up questions, comparing alternatives, testing claims, narrowing options. The evaluation unfolds through the exchange itself.

In this conversational journey, each exchange forms what can be called a **turn**. The initial question and answer are **Turn 1**. The first follow-up exchange becomes **Turn 2**. If the consumer continues probing, comparing, and refining the decision, the interaction becomes **multi-turn**. The decision journey that once required multiple clicks across multiple sites can now unfold entirely within a single conversational thread.

Click-Through still exists. In fact, many large language models are beginning to integrate shopping tools that allow users to "click to buy" directly within the chat interface itself. But the role of the click is changing. Increasingly, the evaluation process happens before that moment—inside the answer.

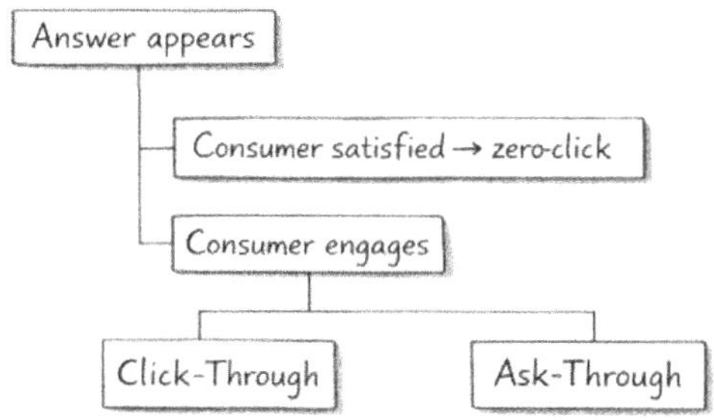


The shift from clicks to questions, from pages to answers, and from navigation to conversation reshapes how consumers discover, evaluate, and ultimately choose brands. The shift also creates a new kind of visibility problem. Brands that once competed to be clicked must now compete to be *answered*.

This chapter focuses on the Ask-Through: what the Ask-Through model demands and why most organizations are structurally unprepared for it. As consumers increasingly ask AI systems questions about products, safety, ingredients, sustainability, and performance, a gap emerges between what consumers want answered and what brands have explained in clear, accessible ways.

This chapter also disrupts the *conversion funnel*—the traditional marketing model that tracks a consumer's progression from initial awareness through consideration to purchase. The funnel assumed demand unfolded gradually, across multiple touchpoints, each of which a marketer could observe and influence. In the Ask-Through, that sequence is compressed dramatically. The consideration phase that once unfolded across days or weeks now collapses into the span of a conversation.

## How AI Compresses the Consumer Journey

For decades, demand revealed itself gradually. Consumers moved from awareness to interest, from interest to consideration, and from consideration to purchase. Marketers inferred intent through proxy signals: keyword volume, impressions—the count of how many times an ad or content unit was displayed—clicks, dwell time, and conversion rates. These proxies worked because decision-making was distributed across time and touchpoints. Each step left a trace, and each trace informed a response.

AI-mediated behavior collapses that process in a way that fundamentally disrupts the model. When consumers ask an AI system a question today, the prompt often contains not just curiosity but decision criteria.

Compare two queries. "Best yoga pants" signals exploration. "Best yoga pants that are squat-proof, durable after washing, and under $120" signals a decision already forming. In the traditional journey, that level of specificity might emerge only after visiting multiple sites. In an AI-mediated journey, it can appear in a single prompt.

AI systems treat decision criteria as instructions rather than suggestions. They do not return a list of links for the consumer to evaluate—they synthesize an answer. They narrow the field. In many cases, they name a winner. A brand's window of influence—the period during which the brand can shape how a consumer thinks—has compressed dramatically. The synthesis happens before the brand ever speaks directly.

The scale of this shift is measurable. Gartner projects that traditional search engine referral traffic will decline by 50 percent by 2028—and many analysts consider that estimate conservative.[1]

### *Why Early Answer Leadership Becomes Hard to Displace*

AI systems do not treat all sources equally over time. AI systems gradually develop source preferences based on the clarity, credibility, and consistency of the information they encounter. When a brand repeatedly provides well-structured answers to common questions, the system becomes more likely to reference that source again in future responses.

The window in which a brand can shape the consumer's thinking has compressed dramatically. As AI-mediated queries displace exploratory search, the brands already recognized as reliable explainers become harder to displace. Early movers are not just winning individual answers—they are shaping the default assumptions AI systems hold about their category. The organizational choice is not whether to build answer infrastructure—the structured, accessible content layer that enables consistent responses across channels. The choice is whether to build it before the pattern solidifies or after someone else's words become the category reference.

## The Ask-Through Funnel: Prompt → Answer → Follow-Up → Confirmation

To understand how this shift changes decision behavior, we need to look at how AI-mediated conversations unfold. Unlike traditional digital funnels that begin with an impression or a click, the Ask-Through journey begins with a **prompt**—a natural-language question posed to an AI system.

The system returns an **answer**, typically synthesized from multiple sources and presented in a confident, contextualized form. If the response resonates, the consumer does not leave the environment. Instead, the interaction continues inside the conversation.

The next stage is **follow-up**. This is where the Ask-Through model diverges most clearly from traditional search behavior. In a Click-Through journey, returning to search results often signals dissatisfaction. In a zero-click interaction, the consumer simply accepts the answer and moves on. In an Ask-Through exchange, however, a follow-up question signals something different: *engagement*. The consumer probes further, asks for clarification, compares alternatives, or tests the strength of the recommendation.

Finally comes **confirmation**. At this stage, the consumer seeks reassurance that the answer holds up. This may involve asking for comparisons between finalists, requesting additional detail, or occasionally visiting a product page to verify a claim. The decision process unfolds across multiple conversational turns rather than across multiple websites.

Because of this structure, Ask-Through surfaces very different signals from the Click-Through model:

- **Scrutiny, not traffic.** Does the answer hold up when the consumer probes further? Does the brand survive Turn 2?
- **Resilience, not reach.** Do consumers continue asking questions about the brand, or does the conversation move elsewhere?
- **Multi-turn depth, not single-turn volume.** Performance across a multi-turn conversation is becoming a stronger indicator of trust than click-through rate alone.

The Click-Through rewarded attention. Ask-Through rewards resilience—the ability to hold up when the consumer asks again. Designing for Ask-Through means designing for the conversation, not just the conversion.

### *Why Turn 2 Is Where Brands Lose Control*

The first answer in an AI conversation is often manageable. AI systems draw on a brand's published content, third-party reviews, news coverage, and official documentation. If a brand has strong foundational content—clear, consistent, and well-sourced—the brand tends to survive Turn 1 reasonably intact. Turn 2 is where brands lose control.

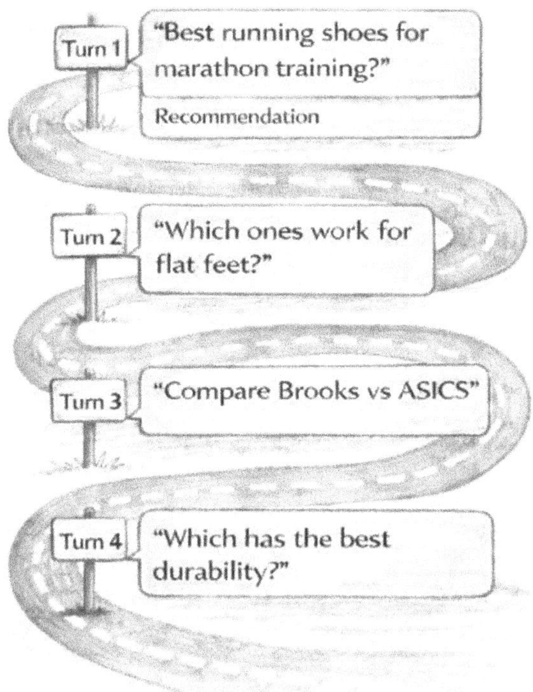


Follow-up questions—"But are there any safety concerns?" or "What do people actually complain about?" or "Is that claim independently verified?"—invite the AI to surface what the brand has not addressed. Nuance, handled by AI systems with care, triggers more nuance. The AI does not inflate claims under questioning. It surfaces tension. When a brand has left questions unanswered, or answered them inconsistently across channels, the AI constructs its response from whatever credible external sources are available: reviews, forums, regulatory filings, competitor commentary.

This Turn 2 vulnerability has concrete commercial implications. Alexa for Shopping's AI assistant, which sits at the precise intersection of question and purchase, illustrates the pattern clearly. According to Amazon's Q3 2025 earnings call, roughly 60 percent of consumers who ask a question through Alexa for Shopping go on to purchase more product.[2] Asking does not slow conversion. In many cases, it accelerates it.

The reason is straightforward: A question signals engagement, intent, and readiness. When answered clearly and honestly, a question reduces uncertainty—the single greatest inhibitor of action. The Ask-Through works because it meets consumers where they actually are: curious, not yet decided, and looking for a reason to commit.

The same dynamic that accelerates conversion for brands with strong answer infrastructure can redirect consumers toward alternatives when a brand's answers are absent, inconsistent, or unconvincing. The question is asked regardless. The answer comes from somewhere.

## The Answer Divide

Most brands are not built for the Ask-Through. Not because they lack capability, but because they were deliberately designed to do the opposite: to manage questions down, not answer them up. To understand why, it helps to name the divide that AI has now made visible—the Answer Divide.

### *Two Experiences of "Help"*

When people interact with AI answer engines—ChatGPT, Claude, Gemini, or Perplexity—they encounter a posture that feels fundamentally different from most brand interactions. These systems are designed around *inquiry*. They invite questions in natural language. They listen without visible agenda. They explain patiently. They acknowledge uncertainty. They surface trade-offs instead of hiding them. The experience feels less like marketing and more like guidance—less like persuasion and more like service.

Now compare that experience with a typical brand-owned environment. Brand websites and apps are still primarily engineered for *control*. Navigation is curated. Journeys are optimized. Messaging is staged. Uncertainty is smoothed over. Questions that complicate the sale are often buried, delayed, or reframed. The underlying assumption remains largely unchanged: Questions create friction, and friction threatens conversion.

The differences between AI agents and brand environments are stark:

- **AI agents deliver:** 24/7 availability, empathetic conversational tone, openly surfaced trade-offs, responses personalized to stated context, no commercial agenda, and multi-turn depth that deepens with each follow-up question
- **Brand environments deliver:** Curated navigation, staged promotional messaging, suppressed uncertainty, friction engineered at the inquiry layer, and optimization toward a single conversion exit

The contrast is not marginal. It is structural. It is not about interface aesthetics or copywriting tone. It reflects two fundamentally different philosophies about the role of questions in decision-making. AI systems treat inquiry as the point of value. Most brands still treat inquiry as something to be managed or interrupted.

The gap between those two philosophies is what can be called the **Answer Divide**: the space between what consumers need to know and what brands make knowable. The divide compounds when internal functions operate independently. Marketing crafts aspiration. Legal minimizes liability. Product documents functionality. Customer support handles edge cases. No single function owns the coherent answer layer. AI systems don't respect those silos—they integrate all surfaces and expose contradictions.

The failure mode is clearest in regulated categories. In consumer financial services, owned content often emphasizes simplicity and ease of account opening—but the questions consumers carry are documented not in marketing materials, but in call-center logs, regulatory filings, and consumer complaint databases: overdraft fee thresholds, account closure procedures, dispute timelines, hidden charges in promotional rates.[3]

AI systems ingest all of it. The answer consumers receive reflects the full record, not the preferred tagline. Brands that have not answered their own hard questions discover that those questions have been answered anyway—from external sources built for accuracy, not brand preference.

Pharmaceutical OTC products face a structurally similar problem. Brand content emphasizes efficacy and tolerability. Consumer questions about drug interactions, appropriate dosing for edge cases, long-term use patterns, and discontinuation effects are answered inconsistently—or not at all—across owned surfaces. The AI draws on clinical literature, FDA labeling, formulary databases, and forum discussions. None of it was written to serve a brand's commercial interest. Brands lose not because AI behaves unfairly, but because unanswered questions surface the gap between what was claimed and what was documented.

### *The Habit Shift No Dashboard Shows*

As AI-mediated inquiry becomes routine, consumer behavior is shifting in a way most marketing analytics systems are not built to detect. Web traffic metrics do not register the queries consumers are directing at AI systems before they visit a brand site. Impression counts do not capture the consideration phases now resolved in a chat window. Conversion rates can appear stable—because the consumers still arriving are more decided—but the consumers who would have arrived through exploratory intent are no longer coming at all. The consideration phase has moved offsite, and it left no forwarding address.

There is no cliff in the analytics dashboard. The erosion is structural and gradual. Brands are not losing sudden traffic drops—they are losing the early stages of the decision cycle, one AI-resolved query at a time. By the time the pattern becomes visible in owned-channel metrics, the pattern has already compounded. The consumers still arriving have already decided. The consumers who might have been persuaded have already been answered—by someone else.

### *How the Cost-Center Model Created the Answer Divide*

To understand why the Answer Divide runs so deep inside large organizations, consider where questions historically lived.

For decades, anything related to answering consumer questions—call centers, customer service teams, help desks, support forums—was treated not as a strategic capability, but as a non-strategic cost center. The mandate was defensive, not generative. The goals were widely shared and rarely questioned:

- Fewer consumers through the support pipeline
- Less time spent per consumer
- Faster resolution, not better explanation

Success was measured in containment, deflection, and efficiency. The best outcome was often no interaction at all. This logic shaped incentives far beyond service organizations. Marketing learned to persuade without inviting questions. Legal learned to minimize exposure rather than enable understanding. Product teams shipped features without fully explaining trade-offs. Over time, inquiry itself became something to manage down.

AI has now flipped the economics of that equation. Questions are no longer scarce or expensive. They are low-friction, private, judgment-free, machine-mediated, and infinitely reusable. Consumers can ask what they want to know, not what a dropdown menu anticipates. They can probe uncertainty without triggering a sales response. They can ask follow-ups without penalty. And once that experience becomes normal, expectations reset permanently.

Consumers don't decide that brand websites are "bad." They simply stop needing them at the moment of inquiry. This quiet substitution is how the Answer Divide takes hold—not through backlash or rejection, but through gradual bypass. Loyalty erosion in the Answer Economy rarely looks like churn. It looks like absence. Brands are not rejected; they are bypassed. And because the bypass happens before any owned-channel metric fires, the only way to see the pattern coming is to audit the questions consumers are already asking AI systems—and compare that list to the questions your brand has answered clearly, publicly, and consistently.

## Answer Media: The New Front Page

Twenty years ago, while building one of the first social listening companies, I coined the term "Consumer-Generated Media"[4] (CGM) to describe how customer conversations functioned as media—shaping perception, driving decisions, and commanding attention just like traditional outlets, whether marketers paid for them or not. We are at a similar inflection point today.

The most valuable impression in the Answer Economy is no longer an ad or a post. It is what answer engines say about your brand when consumers ask. This is **Answer Media**—the synthesized responses that inform, influence, and shape decisions at the moment they matter most.

Answer engines have become de facto media because they filter and frame information just as traditional outlets once did. But unlike traditional media—where a brand could buy placement or pitch coverage—Answer Media requires something more fundamental: A brand must deserve inclusion through credibility, clarity, and evidence.

The result is a zero-click information environment—one in which users increasingly consume answers without visiting any external link at all. When an AI system responds to "What's the best air purifier for allergies?" or "Is this supplement safe during pregnancy?" the answer is delivered complete, synthesized from multiple sources, blended into a single authoritative response. The user never visits the brand's site, never sees the brand's ad, never reads the brand's content directly. The implication is direct: If a brand is not in the answer, the answer has already moved on without the brand.

This zero-click reality creates an uncomfortable reckoning: Decades of search-engine optimization were built on the premise that visibility meant ranking in a list of links. That premise is breaking. The new visibility challenge is whether a brand is mentioned in the answer at all—and how the brand is characterized when it is.

### *Answer Media at the Moment of Purchase*

The Alexa for Shopping data introduced earlier in this chapter—where 60 percent of consumers who ask a question go on to purchase more product—plays out most consequentially at the retail layer, where AI synthesis and purchase decision happen in a single interface. A consumer entering a category conversation at the "What's the healthiest cereal for my child?" level receives synthesized guidance that narrows options before any brand messaging appears. The brand's owned content matters, but only as one ingredient in a synthesis process the brand does not control.

Answer Media's power comes from its apparent objectivity—or more precisely, from the perception that the system is optimizing for the user's interests rather than a brand's commercial agenda. Brands that understand the shift from persuading to informing are better positioned. Brands that resist the shift discover that their competitors or private labels already occupy the answer.

Unlike traditional media, where placement could be purchased and the message controlled, Answer Media operates on a fundamentally different logic: Answers earn their position through trust signals accumulated over time. Reviews, third-party coverage, consistent brand content, and clear explanations of trade-offs all feed the system. The moment commercial motivation appears to bias the synthesis, trust collapses.

### *From Containment to Capability*

Once answers are recognized as media—not rhetorically, but economically—the internal conversation inside organizations begins to change. Instead of asking how to reduce question volume, leaders can ask which questions correlate most strongly with conversion, where unanswered questions stall decisions, and which answers perform best across AI platforms and purchase journeys.

Answer Media becomes the connective tissue between service, marketing, and commerce. Answer Media reframes explanation as a growth lever rather than a liability and aligns naturally with how AI systems allocate influence. Most brand websites are optimized to sell, not to explain. But AI systems do not reward closure. They reward clarity under questioning.

When an answer engine evaluates a brand, the system is not asking whether the messaging is compelling or differentiated. The system is asking whether the brand can be confidently explained, whether trade-offs are acknowledged, whether information is consistent across sources, and whether recommending the brand introduces risk. The practical starting point is the same for every organization: Identify the twenty or thirty questions consumers are most likely to ask an AI system about the category, check how the brand currently appears in the answers, and assess where the gap between what the brand claims and what the AI finds is largest. That gap is where Answer Media work begins.

Brand leaders must treat Answer Media as a distinct planning category alongside social, paid display, and traditional search. That means auditing which questions the brand already answers well, identifying the gaps that third parties are filling, and building the organizational capability to answer consistently—at scale, across every platform where consumers ask.

## Question Coverage and the Cost of Silence

In the Ask-Through economy, the most dangerous gap is not the one consumers see—it is the one they do not realize exists. When a consumer asks an AI system a question and receives a confident, synthesized answer, that consumer rarely knows that the brand at the center of the response never wrote a single word of it. The AI did not fabricate anything. The AI assembled the most credible content available. And if that content came from a regulatory complaint, a Reddit thread, or a competitor's comparison page—that is the answer the consumer received. The consequence of failing to build Question Coverage is straightforward: AI systems assemble answers from the most credible sources available, whether or not the brand is among them.

**Question Coverage** is a brand's ability to clearly, consistently, and publicly answer the questions consumers are most likely to bring to AI systems about the brand's category and products. Question Coverage is not a metric. It is a capability—the organizational commitment to building an answer layer broad enough to cover the decision surface that AI systems now traverse on a consumer's behalf. The brand that has invested in Question Coverage does not merely rank better in AI responses. The brand's own voice shapes the synthesis.

### *Pattern Lock-In and the Hardening Narrative*

Most brands discover their Question Coverage gap too late—after the AI has already settled into a narrative the brand did not write. This process—where repeated answers harden into the default narrative—is known as **pattern lock-in**.

Pattern lock-in does not require hostile intent. Pattern lock-in requires only persistence. If a supplement brand has failed to clearly answer "Is this product safe for long-term use?"—the question will be answered anyway, by PubMed abstracts, by FDA labeling guidance, by archived posts from a pharmacist-run forum thread that has accumulated thousands of upvotes over two years. The AI does not weight those sources by brand preference. The AI weights them by credibility signals: author authority, citation density, consistency across sources, and recency. A brand's own content, if thin or aspirational, simply loses the field—not in one visible defeat, but in thousands of individual queries, quietly, over time.

The window for reversing pattern lock-in is not closed. But the window narrows with each passing quarter of silence. The brands that act before a narrative hardens pay the *cost of building*. The brands that act after pay the *cost of displacement*—which is higher, slower, and never fully complete.

### *Where Silence Creates the Most Risk*

Not all unanswered questions carry equal weight. Three categories consistently produce the highest pattern lock-in risk: (1) supplement and wellness brands, (2) home security and smart device brands, and (3) premium apparel and activewear brands.

Supplement and wellness brands operate in a category where consumer questions cluster around safety, efficacy, and interaction risks—precisely the questions brand content most often avoids. A consumer asking, "Can I take this supplement with blood pressure medication?" or "Is this brand third-party tested?" will not find the answer in aspirational copy about natural ingredients and energy support. The AI will find the answer in a pharmacist's blog post, a clinical review abstract, or a warning letter in the FDA's public database. Brands that have answered these questions plainly—with clinical references, third-party certifications, and clearly stated contraindications—occupy the answer. Brands that have not are absent from the most consequential conversation happening about their product.

Home security and smart device brands face a structurally similar exposure around privacy and law enforcement access. A consumer asking, "Does this brand share footage with police?" or "Who has access to my home camera feed?" is asking a question the typical brand FAQ section rarely addresses clearly. The AI draws from investigative journalism, EFF privacy analyses, and state attorney general guidance.[5] The brand that has answered these questions publicly—with explicit data-sharing policies, opt-in and opt-out language, and published transparency reports—shapes the response. The brand that routes these questions to a legal disclaimer page does not.

Premium apparel and activewear brands carrying sustainability claims face a version of this problem that marketing language alone cannot manage. A consumer asking, "Is this brand actually ethical?" or "Where is this brand manufactured?" will find the answer in labor audit reports, garment worker advocacy publications, and fashion industry watchdog assessments—and those sources are not optimized for brand preference. The brand that has answered these questions with specificity—named manufacturing facilities, published audit results, remediation commitments, fair wage data—competes on its own terms. The brand that has answered them with aspirational language about "our commitment to people and the planet" is not in the conversation at all.

### Case Study: A Premium Activewear Brand Discovers the Gap

Consider a mid-tier activewear brand—leggings, sports bras, and training shorts priced between $60 and $120—that built its business on social media and influencer marketing. The brand has a loyal customer base, a clean aesthetic, and strong creative content. What the brand does not have is a structured answer layer.

When a consumer asks an AI system "Is this brand sustainable?" the system does not surface the brand's sustainability page. The system surfaces a scoring by a textile accountability organization that rates the brand's recycled polyester claims against actual fiber-sourcing data. The system surfaces a forum thread where customers who

(*continued*)

search placement. The platform reinforces that behavior through search ranking. The result is an environment where explanation is structurally rewarded, not managed down.

Airbnb operates on a similar logic. Every listing is a structured answer to the questions a traveler has: What does the space look like? What are the rules? What do previous guests actually say? What happens if something goes wrong? Hosts who earn Superhost status do so partly through response metrics—not just star ratings. The platform actively surfaces hosts who answer questions before those questions are asked, through detailed house manuals, arrival guides, and explicit exception policies. That documentation prevents the three-star review; the documentation is also precisely what AI systems look for when evaluating whether to recommend a stay.

In many ways, Etsy and Airbnb already behaved like large language models—listening, responding, adapting—long before LLMs entered the mainstream. The result is deeper trust. When AI systems evaluate these platforms, the systems find environments already optimized for explanation rather than persuasion.

### *Colgate-Palmolive: The Living FAQ*

The Colgate-Palmolive corporate homepage functions less like a promotional front door and more like a structured resource for consumers with real questions. The site makes it remarkably easy to get clear answers about oral care, ingredient safety, usage, and sustainability. Colgate maintains an ingredient glossary, age-by-age oral care guidance, and plain-language answers to questions about fluoride safety that the category has fielded for decades. None of the content is buried in an FAQ tab—the content surfaces through the same navigation used to reach product recommendations.

This posture is not accidental. The posture reflects a deliberate organizational choice to prioritize explanation over aspiration. The practical consequence is that when an AI system processes a consumer question about children's toothpaste ingredients or the safety of whitening products, Colgate has already answered the question—clearly, consistently, and in the brand's own voice. The AI does not have to construct a response from fragmentary external sources. The brand's own explanation is structurally available. In a world where AI systems regularly cite brand-owned content when constructing answers, that choice has strategic value.

### *Nestlé: A Decade of Structured Openness*

Long before "answer readiness" entered the marketing vocabulary, Nestlé operationalized the same philosophy through its Ask Nestlé initiative. For nearly a decade, teams inside Nestlé's corporate communications function have treated public questioning not as a risk to be minimized, but as an opportunity to explain the company more fully.

Ask Nestlé spans an unusually broad range of topics: new product formulations, nutrition science, supply-chain sourcing standards, environmental commitments, and responses to consumer concerns. The results have not gone unnoticed.

Nestlé has ranked near the top of the Bowen Craggs Corporate Digital Communications Index for several years, where its Ask Nestlé platform has been recognized as one of the most comprehensive corporate FAQ resources.[6] The initiative has also received broader recognition for building a digital presence designed to project transparency and openness.[7]

The practical outcome is visible in AI-mediated environments. When a consumer asks an AI about Nestlé's use of palm oil, the sourcing standards for its coffee brands, or the nutritional profile of a baby formula, Ask Nestlé has typically already answered the question. The AI does not have to assemble a response from fragmentary external criticism. The brand's own explanation—structured, consistently maintained, and more substantive than most of the critical coverage—is what the system finds first. That is not a communications strategy. It is content architecture that functions as a form of advance reputation insurance.

What Nestlé, Colgate-Palmolive, Etsy, and Airbnb have in common is that each grasped something before most brands did: The synthesized answers AI systems deliver about a brand function as a form of media—and that media must be earned, not bought. That recognition is the starting point for understanding what the Answer Economy actually demands of brand leaders.

## Key Takeaways

- The defining demand signal has shifted from the click to the question. In the Answer Economy, what consumers ask—and how AI systems answer—reveals intent more clearly than impressions, rankings, or click-through rates.

- Click-Through and Ask-Through now coexist. Consumers may click to explore, accept a synthesized answer without leaving the interface, or continue the decision process through multi-turn conversations that refine the answer.
- Brands typically lose narrative control in Turn 2, when follow-up questions surface gaps between brand messaging and external evidence. The first response often reflects brand messaging, but follow-up questions surface nuance, trade-offs, and unanswered concerns drawn from broader sources.
- The Answer Divide reflects how organizations are built, not how AI works. The gap between consumer questions and brand answers typically arises from internal silos where marketing persuades, legal limits exposure, and service handles inquiries separately.
- Question Coverage is becoming the new competitive moat. Brands that consistently answer the hard questions—about safety, sourcing, performance, and trade-offs—shape the synthesis AI systems deliver to consumers.
- If the brand does not answer clearly, AI will—using someone else's words. AI systems assemble the most credible available explanation, whether that content comes from the brand itself, competitors, regulators, or third-party voices.

# 6 The Three Metrics That Matter: Visibility, Vulnerability, and Readiness

**Prompted Moment**

*What happens when a shopper points their phone at your product and asks, "Is this any good?"—before reading your packaging?*

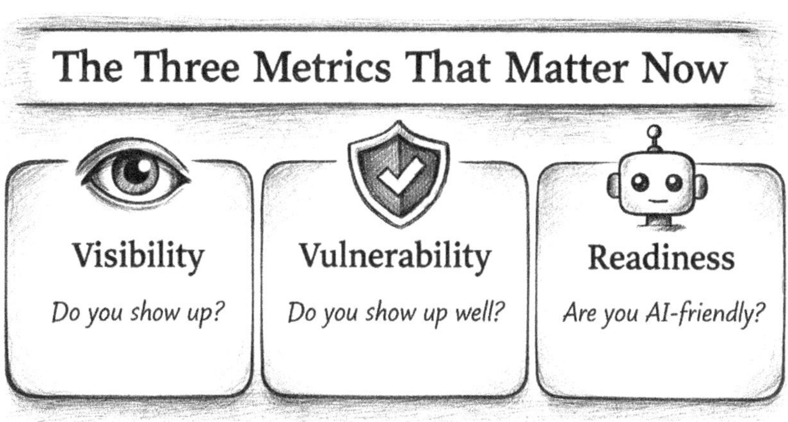

Consumers are beginning to ask machines about brands before they encounter the brands themselves. A shopper standing in a store aisle can now point a phone at a product and ask an AI system whether it is worth buying. A homeowner considering a new appliance can ask which brand is most reliable before visiting a manufacturer's website. A patient researching a medication can ask whether the product is safe before reading the label.

In each case, the first explanation a consumer hears about a brand may not come from the brand at all. It may come from an AI system that has synthesized information about that brand from across the internet. In practical terms, the first interpretation of a brand's reputation may now occur inside an AI-generated answer rather than inside the brand's own marketing.

For decades, marketing influence began with exposure. A consumer saw an advertisement, encountered packaging, visited a website, or heard about a product through word of mouth. Traditional marketing metrics were built around that sequence. Awareness, reach, share of voice, and conversion rates all measure performance once the consumer has already encountered the brand.

AI-mediated answers invert that order. When consumers ask machines for guidance, the system summarizes the category, evaluates competing claims, and presents recommendations before the consumer encounters the brand directly.

The strategic question for leaders becomes straightforward: *How does a brand perform when an AI system interprets its reputation before the consumer sees its marketing?*

Three metrics—Visibility, Vulnerability, and Readiness—allow leaders to measure how brands perform when AI systems increasingly mediate consumer judgment. Together, they provide a practical scoreboard for an environment where machines summarize brand reputations before humans encounter them.

In paid media, a brand controlled the message but not the audience. In earned media, a brand influenced the message but could not guarantee placement. In Answer Media, brands cannot control what AI systems ultimately say. What they can influence are the inputs those systems rely on—the documentation, evidence, product information, and third-party signals that AI systems use when constructing answers.

Three metrics have proven most useful to leadership teams navigating the Answer Economy. Together, they form a CEO-level scoreboard built for an environment where machines synthesize brand reputations before humans encounter them:

- **Visibility** measures whether a brand appears when consumers ask high-intent, category-relevant questions across AI answer engines. Visibility is about presence—whether a brand exists, in a meaningful way, inside the answers that shape decisions.
- **Vulnerability** measures whether AI-generated narratives reinforce trust or introduce qualification, distortion, or reputational risk. A brand can be highly visible and still be vulnerable, because what the AI says about it may hedge, qualify, or contradict the brand's own stated position.
- **Readiness** measures whether the organization is structurally prepared to influence future answers—whether its documented truth is accessible, defensible, and machine-usable. Readiness is the only metric a brand can directly act on.

Visibility and Vulnerability describe what AI systems currently say. Readiness determines whether that interpretation is fixed or flexible.

These three metrics operate earlier in the decision process than traditional brand or performance measures. They capture how AI systems shape consumer perception *before* downstream indicators—traffic, conversion, or sales—register any signal.

## Visibility: Is Your Brand in the Answer?

Visibility is the most intuitive of the three metrics—and the most frequently misunderstood. Leaders often assume it resembles traditional share-of-voice measurement: how often a brand appears across a defined set of channels or publications. Visibility is related to that idea, but captures something more specific. Share of voice measures how much a brand is talked about in spaces where people produce content. Visibility measures whether a brand appears in the synthesized answers AI systems return to consumers at the exact moment a decision is being made.

### *What Visibility Actually Measures*

Visibility is measured through structured AI audits. In practice, analysts submit representative consumer questions to major AI answer engines—mirroring how real consumers explore a category, compare options, and evaluate risks. The responses are then evaluated to determine whether the brand appears, where it appears within the answer, and how it is characterized relative to alternatives.

This approach surfaces patterns that keyword ranking and traffic analysis cannot. Brands often appear robustly in informational contexts—"What is this brand known for?"—and go missing in evaluative ones—"What is the best option in this category for someone with this specific constraint?" The evaluative question is where the decision happens. Absence there is the more consequential finding.

Visibility also reveals where a brand appears relative to the answer's structure. Being mentioned in a caveat differs from being named as a recommendation. Being included as an alternative differs from being identified as the preferred choice. VVR scoring distinguishes between these positions because they carry different implications for downstream consumer behavior.

When brands are evaluated against hundreds of real, high-intent consumer questions—comparison questions, reassurance questions, safety questions, "best for me" questions—patterns emerge that channel metrics alone cannot reveal. A brand may dominate awareness and still fail to appear when a consumer asks a machine to help them decide. Visibility, measured this way, becomes a map of decision coverage rather than a scoreboard of exposure. The distinction has commercial consequences: When a brand is absent at the moment a consumer's question is answered, no downstream investment in messaging, packaging, or conversion can recover that opportunity.

### *The Discovery Gap: When Awareness Outpaces AI Presence*

One of the most common findings in Visibility audits is what we call the **Discovery Gap**: the difference between how well consumers know a brand and how often that brand appears in AI-generated answers to decision-oriented questions.

This gap is the Answer Economy's version of a *distribution problem*. Just as a strong brand can have poor shelf presence in a key retail channel, a well-known brand can have poor answer presence in the AI channels where decision-making increasingly begins.

Lululemon illustrates this pattern clearly. A BrandRank.AI analysis in the fourth quarter of 2025 found the brand appearing in seven out of ten AI recommendations across activewear queries overall—a strong aggregate score. But that average concealed a sharp internal contrast between categories where the brand is dominant and categories where it is nearly invisible.

In women's core activewear, Lululemon is close to untouchable. The brand earns a perfect 10.0 on "flattering workout leggings" queries across all six major AI engines, 9.8 on hot yoga apparel, and 9.3 across athleisure brand comparisons. Those are the categories the brand has answered consistently and credibly for years—through fabric innovation in Nulu, Luon, and Everlux; through community programming at 3,000-plus annual events; and through direct-to-consumer depth that AI systems recognize and reward.

The contrast becomes visible when the questions shift away from the brand's historical strengths. On "men's performance wear for running," Lululemon scores 1.2; Nike scores 10.0. On men's hiking apparel, cycling gear, and outdoor performance queries, Lululemon scores 0.0 across thirteen separate query types—this despite men accounting for approximately 24 percent of the brand's revenue. Men's athletic wear averages 4.9 across query categories, making it a category where the brand has strong commercial presence and near-zero AI presence simultaneously.

The gap is starker still when it comes to questions about sustainability. "Be Planet" is Lululemon's central brand commitment to sustainability. On AI queries about sustainable activewear, Lululemon scores 0.8; Adidas scores 7.0 on the same queries. A Canada Competition Bureau greenwashing investigation—combined with quietly revised environmental targets—has left the brand's sustainability positioning nearly invisible at the moment of AI-mediated discovery, regardless of what the brand says in its own materials.[1]

This pattern appears across many premium brands. Companies often build deep authority around their core positioning while leaving nearby categories or use cases less documented—because those adjacent spaces were historically served through advertising, campaigns, and promotional investment rather than through documented, structured evidence. AI systems do not assume relevance beyond what the evidence supports. If documentation does not clearly connect a brand to a particular use case or category, the system simply omits it.

## Vulnerability: Where AI Narratives Introduce Risk

Vulnerability measures the gap between what a brand claims and what AI systems can independently verify. A brand can be highly visible—appearing in many answers—and still be vulnerable, because the AI's characterization hedges, qualifies, or contradicts the brand's own stated position. The practical question Vulnerability answers is not "What is being said about us?" but rather "Where is the evidence supporting our claims limited or inconsistent enough that AI systems hedge their conclusions?"

That reframe matters for how organizations respond. Vulnerability findings are not primarily a communications problem. They are a structural one. The fix is not better messaging—it is closing the gap between what the brand asserts and what the evidence can independently support.

### *Vulnerability Is a Pattern, Not an Incident*

Conventional reputation management treats risk as episodic. Brand equity metrics may dip and recover. A crisis emerges. A response follows. Attention moves on.

AI systems work differently. They do not amplify isolated events. They amplify patterns—and the patterns they detect are not the ones organizations typically monitor.

When Vulnerability is measured across dimensions—safety, transparency, authenticity, sustainability, customer experience—recurring narrative clusters become visible. A brand's AI-generated characterization may consistently hedge on one dimension while performing confidently on others. Those hedges are not random. They reflect the AI system's best assessment of where evidence is thin, where claims are inconsistent across sources, or where consumer-facing documentation doesn't fully corroborate marketing-facing assertions.

Consequently, Vulnerability patterns often persist long after internal remediation. Organizations address the underlying issue—they reformulate a product, change a policy, update a claim—but the evidence of remediation isn't always structured in a way that AI systems can locate and verify. The hedge remains in the synthesized answer because the corroborating evidence hasn't been made machine-accessible. Vulnerability, in this sense, is a signal about where AI systems lack confidence, clarity, or corroboration—not a moral judgment about the brand.

### *Brand Alignment: When AI Evaluates a Brand's Claims*

One of the most revealing signals within Vulnerability analysis is the **Brand Alignment Score**. This score measures how closely an AI system's independent description of a brand aligns with the claims that brand makes about itself.

Most brands promote a clear set of promises—about quality, sustainability, innovation, customer service, or safety. A Brand Alignment Score evaluates whether AI systems reinforce those promises when answering consumer questions.

A high score indicates that the AI system's characterization of the brand supports the brand's stated position. A low score indicates a gap: The system either qualifies the claim, introduces competing evidence, or presents a more cautious interpretation than the brand itself would prefer.

This gap matters because AI systems increasingly act as interpreters of brand reputation. Consumers do not always read brand messaging directly. Instead, they ask AI systems questions such as:

- Is this brand trustworthy?
- Is this product actually good quality?
- Is this company really sustainable?

The answer they receive reflects not just what the brand says about itself, but what the available evidence allows the AI system to conclude.

For that reason, Brand Alignment Scores are measured *per AI platform*. AI systems do not evaluate brands in identical ways. Each system draws from different training data, weighs sources differently, and synthesizes information according to its own design. Differences between engines therefore provide useful signals about where evidence supporting a brand's claims is strong—and where it is contested or incomplete.

## A Clear Example of Brand Alignment in Practice

Amazon provides a useful illustration of how Brand Alignment analysis works.

For decades, Amazon has positioned itself as "Earth's most customer-centric company." The phrase appears repeatedly in shareholder letters, corporate communications, and public statements by leadership. It is one of the most consistent brand claims in modern corporate history.

Brand Alignment analysis evaluates how AI systems interpret that claim when responding to questions about Amazon's business practices. Each engine's responses are examined across dimensions related to customer centricity—such as pricing transparency, seller relationships, customer complaints, return policies, and overall customer experience.

The results are revealing.

Across most platforms, Amazon performs strongly. AI systems consistently recognize the company's strengths in selection, convenience, logistics, and delivery speed. Those advantages are widely documented and strongly reinforced by independent sources.

But the analysis also reveals variation across engines.

In BrandRank.AI's assessment, Anthropic's Claude assigns Amazon its lowest Brand Alignment Score among the major platforms evaluated. Claude's answers tend to introduce more qualification when discussing Amazon's customer-centric reputation. Responses frequently reference tensions between customer convenience and issues such as marketplace seller fees, counterfeit concerns, or labor criticism.

That finding is noteworthy for an unexpected reason: Anthropic is also Amazon's commercial AI partner, and its technology powers Alexa for Shopping's assistant.

The result demonstrates an important principle of AI-mediated reputation: Proximity does not guarantee leniency. AI systems synthesize evidence from across the information environment. Even when companies collaborate commercially, the answers generated by those systems still reflect the evidence those systems can access and verify.

In practice, Brand Alignment analysis rarely produces a single definitive score for a brand. Instead, it reveals a range of interpretations across platforms. When multiple engines consistently reinforce a brand's claims, the underlying evidence base is usually strong and coherent. When engines diverge sharply, the difference often signals uncertainty in the available documentation or conflicting signals in the broader information ecosystem.

For leaders, this variance is not a flaw in AI systems. It is diagnostic. It shows where a brand's claims are firmly supported—and where the evidence available to machines leaves room for doubt.

### *When AI Misinterprets Product Information*

Not all Vulnerability issues arise from gaps between claims and evidence. In some cases, AI systems simply misinterpret or incorrectly summarize product information. These errors—often called **hallucinations**—occur when a language model generates information that is incorrect or unsupported by the source material.

The consequence is sharpest in product utility contexts. Consumers are increasingly turning to AI for guidance once handled by product manuals, support lines, and customer service: how to use a product correctly, which ingredients are safe to combine, how to interpret a dosage or dilution instruction, what a warning label actually means. These are practical, safety-adjacent queries where an incorrect AI-generated answer can cause direct harm to the consumer—and direct liability exposure for the brand.

The risk exists even when the AI is drawing from genuine brand source material. Product documentation migrates poorly to AI synthesis. Instructions unambiguous in a printed manual can become genuinely misleading when an AI selectively summarizes them, combines them with content from a different product in the same line, or loses the conditional logic that makes the guidance safe. A skincare contraindication with sun exposure might be omitted from an AI answer about application. A cleaning product might be described as compatible with surfaces the manufacturer warned against. A supplement's dosage might be reassembled from multiple sources into a recommendation no single source ever made.

These issues are different from the alignment gaps discussed earlier. In those cases, AI systems qualify a brand's claims because the available evidence is weak or inconsistent. Hallucination problems arise for a different reason: The AI misinterprets or recombines information from the brand's own documentation. The underlying facts may be correct, but the way the system summarizes them produces an answer the brand never intended.

The solution is not stronger evidence but clearer documentation. Product instructions, safety guidance, and specifications must be written so they remain accurate when extracted and summarized by AI systems. Clear language and well-structured information reduce the risk of misinterpretation.

## Readiness: Building What Machines Can Use

Readiness measures whether the organization is structurally prepared to influence future answers—whether its documented truth is accessible, defensible, and machine-usable. It is the only VVR metric a brand can directly act on. Visibility and Vulnerability describe what AI systems currently say. Readiness determines whether that interpretation is fixed or flexible.

When organizations first encounter Vulnerability findings, the instinct is usually to update messaging, refresh content, or launch a content initiative. The instinct is understandable—and usually incomplete. The deeper problem is rarely what the content says. The problem is whether the content is accessible to AI systems at all, whether the claims it makes are supported by independently verifiable evidence, and whether terminology is consistent enough across sources for AI systems to synthesize it without distortion.

### *Why Having Information Isn't Enough*

Most organizations assume that if information exists somewhere—on a website, in a report, in a policy document—it is available to AI systems. In practice, that assumption is rarely true.

AI systems don't browse, infer, or fill in gaps the way humans do. They retrieve, evaluate, and summarize based on structure, evidence, and consistency. A claim buried in a PDF without proper metadata may be functionally invisible during synthesis. A specification that uses different terminology on a product page than on a support page may cause the AI to hedge because it can't confidently reconcile the two. An updated policy whose old version remains indexed creates ambiguity the AI resolves through caution.

Consequently, brands can invest heavily in storytelling, design, and messaging and still encounter hesitation in AI-generated answers. The issue is not intent. It is translation. Readiness reframes AI performance from a creative or communications concern into an organizational capability: The ability to express truth in a form machines can reliably interpret.

### *The Three Building Blocks of Readiness*

Readiness rests on three interdependent elements. The framework was first formalized by BrandRank.AI's co-founder, Hank Hudephl, whose work clarified an important reality: Organizations rarely struggle with having information—they struggle with structuring it in ways machines can reliably interpret. The Readiness framework describes the conditions that must exist for AI systems to discover, evaluate, and accurately represent a brand's evidence.

Each element addresses a different barrier between what a company knows internally and what AI systems can actually understand. Importantly, the elements build on one another. When organizations skip a step, their efforts to improve AI visibility rarely produce meaningful results.

- **Availability** determines whether AI systems can reliably find and access the information in the first place. Crawlable pages, structured product attributes, machine-readable formats, and clean technical architecture are prerequisites. Without them, even strong evidence is effectively invisible during AI synthesis. Many organizations attempt to improve the quality or clarity of their content before ensuring it can be discovered at all—and then wonder why nothing changes. If AI systems cannot reliably access the underlying information, the strength of that information is irrelevant.

- **Depth** determines whether the brand's claims can withstand scrutiny once the information is found. AI systems tend to favor explicit, quantified, and corroborated evidence. When supporting documentation is thin—when marketing claims lack independent verification—AI systems hedge or defer to outside sources that may be less favorable. Depth is not about producing more content. It is about strengthening the evidentiary backbone behind what the brand already says.
- **Clarity** determines whether AI systems can summarize that information without distorting its meaning. Consistent terminology, plain language, and alignment across sources reduce the risk of narrative drift. When a brand describes the same attribute in multiple ways across its documentation, AI systems must reconcile those differences on their own—and that reconciliation is where misinterpretation often occurs. Clarity ensures that when AI systems synthesize the available evidence, they reproduce the intended meaning rather than improvising their own.

Taken together, these three elements convert organizational knowledge into machine-interpretable evidence. Readiness is therefore not simply a content exercise. It is an operational capability: the ability of an organization to express what it knows in a form that AI systems can consistently retrieve, verify, and communicate.

### *From Mystery to Causality*

Without Readiness, AI behavior can feel arbitrary. One answer engine recommends a brand confidently while another hedges or omits it altogether, often for reasons that are difficult for the organization to identify. When Readiness is measured, those differences become easier to interpret. Leaders can trace AI responses back to specific structural causes—missing documentation, inconsistent terminology, inaccessible formats, or thin supporting evidence.

What once appeared unpredictable becomes diagnosable. The gap between what a brand believes it communicates and what AI systems actually extract turns from a mystery into a management problem. This is the shift that converts VVR from a measurement exercise into an operating discipline. When leaders understand their Readiness score, they can prioritize the structural improvements most likely to increase Visibility and reduce Vulnerability over time.

## How Visibility, Vulnerability, and Readiness Work as a System

VVR is most powerful when the three metrics are used together. Each measures a different aspect of how AI systems interpret a brand, and their interaction reveals organizational dynamics that no single metric can expose.

Visibility without Vulnerability monitoring provides only a partial picture. A brand may appear frequently in AI-generated answers and interpret that presence as success. But Vulnerability analysis may reveal that those answers consistently qualify or question the brand's most important claims. In such a case, high Visibility is not necessarily a win—it simply means the brand is present in the conversation while the narrative surrounding it remains uncertain.

Readiness without Visibility and Vulnerability monitoring removes the feedback loop. An organization can make significant structural improvements—better schema, deeper corroboration, cleaner terminology—and still not know whether those improvements are moving the needle in actual AI-generated answers. Visibility and Vulnerability provide the outcome measures that tell leaders whether Readiness investments are working.

*Visibility tells you whether you are in the game. Vulnerability tells you whether being in the game is helping. Readiness tells you what you can actually do about it.*

Walmart offers a clear illustration of how gaps between Readiness and Visibility can appear even at massive scale. In BrandRank.AI's analysis, Walmart earned a Content Readiness score of 7.1, reflecting strong technical accessibility across availability, clarity, and site architecture. In practical terms, this means AI systems can easily locate Walmart's digital content, crawl its product information, and parse the material needed to generate answers.

Yet Walmart's AI Visibility score is only 3.8. Across the set of retail-related questions analyzed, the brand appeared in approximately 61 percent of AI-generated answers, but it was identified as the leading recommendation in only 18 percent of those responses. Amazon, by comparison, appeared in 75 percent of the same queries and was identified as the primary recommendation in 42 percent.

The gap suggests that discoverability alone is not enough. AI systems can find Walmart's information, but the evidence available to them does not consistently position the company as the strongest answer to the question being asked.

The pattern becomes particularly visible in sustainability-related queries. Walmart's Project Gigaton initiative achieved more than one billion metric tons of emissions reductions across its supply chain six years ahead of schedule—a significant and well-documented milestone in corporate environmental efforts. Yet on AI queries about sustainable retail practices, Walmart receives a dismal average score of 0.9 out of 10.

The achievement itself is not in question. The problem is how the supporting evidence is structured. Much of the documentation behind Project Gigaton exists in sustainability reports, partner disclosures, and technical documents that AI systems do not easily synthesize into concise answers about environmentally responsible retailers.

Without Readiness analysis, the resulting gap might appear to be a messaging problem. With it, the issue becomes clearer: The underlying achievement is real, but the supporting evidence has not been assembled in a form that AI systems can easily retrieve, corroborate, and summarize. In this case, the solution is not advertising or brand storytelling. It is improving the structure and accessibility of the documentation that already exists.

For leadership teams, as Walmart's experience suggests, a single AI audit is insufficient. VVR is a monitoring discipline, not a point-in-time assessment. Answer engines update. New content enters the training environment. Brand actions—and competitor actions—create new signals that shift synthesis outputs over time. The brands that manage AI performance most effectively treat VVR as a quarterly board-level KPI (key performance indicator), not an annual agency deliverable.

AI systems don't evaluate campaigns in isolation. They evaluate patterns across the entire organization: what marketing says, what product documentation supports, what policies allow, what customer experiences reinforce, and what third-party sources confirm. The result is a synthesis of organizational behavior, not a marketing score. Many of the most consequential inputs to AI-generated answers—regulatory filings, complaint databases, clinical documentation, seller policies—are produced entirely outside the marketing function.

Visibility shows where marketing has successfully anticipated the questions consumers are asking AI systems. Vulnerability reveals where the brand's claims are qualified or challenged because the supporting evidence across the organization is incomplete or inconsistent. Readiness determines whether the company's documented evidence is structured in a way that allows AI systems to interpret and reproduce the brand's intended message accurately.

## VVR Analysis in Practice

Together, the VVR metrics act as practical mirrors. They reveal where marketing is reinforced by the rest of the organization—and where it is unintentionally weakened by gaps in documentation, evidence, or internal alignment. In the Answer Economy, marketing does not simply tell the story. It inherits the consequences of how well the organization supports that story with verifiable, accessible evidence. The following case illustrates how VVR analysis works in practice.

A national consumer brand debated AI strategy for three quarters without resolution. Marketing advocated for an AI-first content strategy. IT proposed enterprise AI licensing. Legal warned about liability. Finance questioned ROI. No consensus emerged—because no shared measurement framework existed. Each function was arguing from its own definition of the problem, and the conversation cycled without resolution.

In the face of this executive stalemate, the company decided to conduct a VVR diagnostic. Here is what they found:

- **Visibility:** The brand appeared in only 23 percent of category-entry questions despite 78 percent aided awareness. The brand was well known. It was not well answered. AI systems were returning responses in the brand's core category that named alternatives or described the category without the brand appearing at all.
- **Vulnerability:** When the brand did appear, 41 percent of responses included hedging language about claims the marketing team considered core differentiators. The hedges were concentrated on specific

claims—efficacy language, sustainability assertions, customer experience promises—that had strong marketing support but thin independent corroboration.

- **Readiness:** A technical audit revealed documentation fragmentation across the organization. Product specifications lived in PDF formats that AI agents rarely accessed. FAQ structure did not match consumer question patterns. Cross-functional terminology conflicts—different names for the same attribute in marketing, product, and legal documents—were creating synthesis uncertainty the AI resolved through caution.

The diagnostic did not resolve philosophical differences. It created a shared reality. Within ninety days, the organization had established a unified product truth repository owned jointly by product and legal, an answer governance council convened by the CMO with cross-functional authority, and quarterly VVR tracking as a board-level KPI.

The outcome was not primarily technical. It was organizational. The metrics created a language that allowed functions with different priorities and different definitions of risk to argue about the same facts. Achieving that alignment is not possible through discussion alone.

## Key Takeaways

- VVR is a CEO-level measurement framework for the Answer Economy. Visibility, Vulnerability, and Readiness measure brand performance at the layer where AI systems shape consumer decisions—before traditional metrics register any signal at all.
- Visibility is decision coverage, not exposure. A brand may have high awareness and low AI presence. Appearing in 23 percent of relevant answers despite 78 percent aided awareness is an Answer Economy distribution problem, not a messaging one.
- Vulnerability is a pattern, not an incident. AI systems amplify narrative patterns, not isolated events. A low Brand Alignment Score signals that the gap between what a brand asserts and what the evidence can independently support is large enough for AI systems to hedge.

- Proximity does not guarantee leniency. Amazon's weakest Brand Alignment Score comes from Anthropic's Claude—the technology that powers Amazon's own Alexa for Shopping assistant. AI systems evaluate the evidence, not the relationship.
- Readiness is the only metric a brand can directly control. Availability, Depth, and Clarity must be built in sequence. Organizations that improve messaging without establishing evidence access are solving the wrong problem.
- VVR creates organizational alignment where opinion cannot. The VVR diagnostic converts AI from an opinion topic to a governance requirement by giving functions with different priorities a shared set of facts to argue about.
- AI reputation is managed through evidence, not communications. The question is not what story you tell. It is whether the evidence you make accessible to machines supports the story you intend to tell.

# 7 The LATCH Framework: Five Behaviors That Build Trust at Scale

**Prompted Moment**

*If an AI summarized your brand tomorrow based only on what you've done—not what you've said—would you be proud of what it found?*

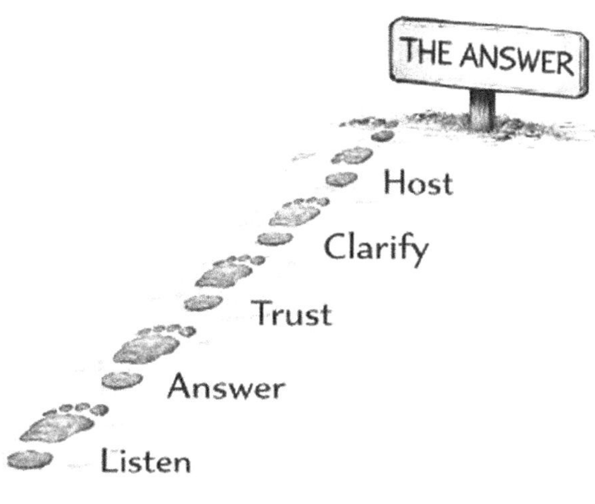


The Behavioral Trail

In Chapter 6, we introduced you to VVR—a way to assess a brand's position in the Answer Economy through Visibility, Vulnerability, and Readiness. Those metrics help diagnose how a brand is likely to appear when people turn to AI for answers.

But measurement alone doesn't change outcomes. The question leaders inevitably ask is simple: What should we do to improve how our brand shows up in AI-generated answers?

This chapter answers that question. It introduces LATCH, a behavioral framework that helps brands strengthen Visibility, reduce their Vulnerability, and build lasting Readiness for an AI-mediated world.

## Why Brands Need to Act Now

AI systems increasingly rely on patterns they observe across the web. When the same credible information appears repeatedly across trusted sources, those systems learn to treat it as reliable content. Over time, those patterns become harder to change as AI systems develop *citation patterns*—tendencies to repeatedly draw on sources and framings they have encountered consistently across the web.

Brands that adopted answer engine optimization (AEO) frameworks in 2024 now show up 40 percent higher in generative AI search results than competitors who waited.[1] Early awareness gives you time to amplify positive narratives before they calcify into the answers AI systems repeat by default.[2]

The shift is already visible. For example, financial publisher NerdWallet has reported declining search traffic in some areas as AI-generated answers increasingly summarize financial advice directly within search results.[3] At the same time, the visitors who do arrive often come with more specific questions and stronger intent. Discovery is moving away from long lists of search results and toward summarized answers.

## Introducing LATCH: A Behavioral Operating System

LATCH is a simple framework describing five behaviors that help brands remain credible and visible as AI systems increasingly mediate information.

The framework is simple to remember, but difficult to live:

- **Listen.** Start with the question, not the message.
- **Answer.** Be useful before you are impressive.
- **Tell the Truth.** Make reality your strongest asset.
- **Clarify.** Turn complexity into confidence.
- **Host.** Stay present in the hard conversations.

Each of these verbs describes something a brand does repeatedly, not something it claims to believe. Together, they form a behavioral profile that AI systems—and people—can recognize, trust, and rely on.

LATCH is not about controlling answers. It's about deserving them.

The behaviors are not independent. They are sequential and cumulative. You cannot Answer well without first Listening—knowing what the question actually is, in the language the customer uses, shaped by the fears they carry. You cannot Tell the Truth credibly without answering first—because truth without utility is just disclosure. Clarify depends on honesty: You can only organize complexity clearly if you are not hiding parts of it. And Hosting—staying present in the hard conversations—requires all four preceding behaviors as its foundation. A brand that skips to hosting without the others will be exposed quickly.

LATCH, practiced in sequence, compounds. Each behavior reinforces the next and strengthens the whole.

## Listen: Start with the Question, Not the Message

Listening means understanding the real questions people ask before deciding what message to push. In the Answer Economy, those questions are increasingly visible through prompts, follow-ups, and conversational searches.

My professional life has been shaped by a persistent inversion: What happens when you let consumers speak first?

At Procter & Gamble, respecting the consumer voice meant building early digital programs that didn't just broadcast messages but absorbed input. The Tide Stain Detective didn't tell people why Tide was great; it answered the question consumers were already asking: How do I get this stain out of this fabric? The Pampers Parenting Institute didn't lead with brand purpose; it addressed late-night anxieties about babies.

At PlanetFeedback, listening was the entire point. The platform existed to let people speak in their own words—to tell their stories, lodge complaints, and demand accountability. Some companies leaned in. Others avoided the noise. The difference in outcomes was stark.

At Nestlé, listening meant sitting in rooms where people read aloud what activists, parents, and critics were saying online—uncurated and uncomfortable. It meant treating patterns not as PR problems, but as signals of misalignment.

In the Answer Economy, listening acquires a new dimension. When someone asks an AI assistant whether your product is safe, how it compares to a competitor, or whether it's worth the price, that question leaves a trace. Patterns emerge across millions of similar queries. AI systems are already reading them. Great brands must learn to reach those patterns too—and then ask themselves the uncomfortable internal questions that surface as a result:

- What fears keep resurfacing?
- What shortcuts are people seeking?
- What comparisons do they insist on making?

Prompts are becoming the new focus groups. They reveal the real language people use when seeking answers. Patterns of answers are the new tracking study. Great brands don't guess. They go where the questions live, and they listen until they are slightly uncomfortable. That discomfort is the signal that reality has drifted beyond the tidy narratives of the annual plan.

When brands fail to listen, critics, competitors, and frustrated customers often end up defining the brand narrative instead. A brand that doesn't listen gets characterized by its critics and its competitors because someone is always willing to fill the silence. The questions people ask AI about your brand do not stop being asked simply because your company hasn't read them. They accumulate, get answered by inference, and harden into the narrative that agents repeat at scale.

## Answer: Be Useful Before You Are Impressive

Answering means providing clear, useful explanations that directly address the questions people are asking. The most effective early digital programs succeeded because they helped people solve specific problems. They explained complicated topics in clear, practice language.

Then digital became a reach channel. Answers were relegated to defensive FAQs written in legalese. Usefulness became secondary to persuasion.

AI reverses that hierarchy.

Agents are extraordinarily good at answering questions. If your brand content cannot match or exceed the clarity, empathy, and specificity of a well-constructed AI response, people will stop coming to you directly.

Brands that truly embody "Answer" as a discipline reorganize around it. They design experiences around real questions. They mine customer service interactions for patterns. They treat clarity as a product feature, not a compliance requirement.

Most importantly, they accept that usefulness comes before persuasion. Emotional resonance still matters, but it cannot compensate for unanswered questions.

If you cannot answer what the brand or product does, who it's for, whether it's safe, and how it compares, you are not in the answer business. You are in the mood business—communicating atmosphere instead of information.

### Case Study: HubSpot

HubSpot did not become one of the most AI-visible B2B brands in the world outspending competitors. It did so by out-answering them.

In a category crowded with software programs making nearly identical claims, HubSpot made a different bet: that the most useful company in the room would eventually own the room. Over more than a decade, HubSpot built the most comprehensive library of marketing and sales education available online—not gated, not buried, not optimized for conversation and the expense of clarity. Just useful, in plain language, at scale.

*(continued)*

*(continued)*

When large language models began generating answers about marketing technology, HubSpot had thousands of explanations to draw from. The brand had essentially pre-answered the answers buyers would one day ask AI. By 2025, HubSpot consistently outperformed category competitors in AI-generated responses—not because it dominated keyword rankings, but because it built the clearest, most consistent record of genuine usefulness across a decade of public content.

The lesson from HubSpot's strategy is not simply about publishing more content. It's about intent. HubSpot built its content library to serve the reader, not to game a system. In the Answer Economy, serving readers and becoming visible to AI systems turn out to be the same thing.[4]

The risk for brands that rely on persuasion is equally instructive. Brands that treat their digital presence as a persuasion channel—brand stories, vision statements, emotional campaigns—find themselves invisible or misrepresented in AI answers, because agents have nothing concrete to cite.

## Tell the Truth: Make Reality Your Strongest Asset

"Telling the truth" sounds like a platitude until you try to practice it at scale. In my early years at Nestlé, we saw what happens when public sustainability messaging moves faster than operational reality. Critics began pointing to inconsistencies between the company's environmental commitments and the pace of measurable change in sourcing and packaging processes. Journalists, activists, and watchdog groups documented these gaps publicly. Once those critiques were indexed by search engines and summarized on platforms like Wikipedia, the narrative became persistent. Rebuilding credibility required years of alignment across sourcing standards, supply-chain reporting, and public communication.

At the Better Business Bureau, truth-telling is the operating system. Companies make claims; consumers test them. The organizations that thrived were the ones that realized it was cheaper, in every sense, to align claims with reality than to litigate exceptions indefinitely.

In the Answer Economy, truth has three concrete dimensions:

1. **Verification.** Claims must be grounded in evidence that can be accessed and cited. "Doctor recommended" must mean something. "Eco-friendly" must be defined.
2. **Candor.** Trade-offs and limitations should be explained, not hidden. Agents will surface them anyway. You might as well participate in the explanation.
3. **Learning.** When you improve something because of feedback or failure, say so. Models train on public artifacts. Progress matters.

In 2011, Patagonia ran a Black Friday advertisement in the *New York Times* with a headline most brands would never dare publish: "Don't Buy This Jacket." The ad acknowledged that even its own products carry an environmental cost—backed by specific water usage figures, carbon impact estimates, and waste statistics for the jacket's production.[5]

Patagonia didn't optimize for AI. They told the truth, consistently, for fourteen years—and the record has been compounding ever since. By 2025, Patagonia held the highest "Answer Share" in the sustainable outdoor apparel category, not because it outspent competitors, but because third parties would not stop validating the company's claims. For Patagonia, AI systems have an abundance of consistent, corroborated material to draw from.[6]

The brand that tells the uncomfortable truth ends up with the most durable record, and in the Answer Economy, the record is the brand. Truth-telling doesn't make you immune to scrutiny. But it changes the nature of that scrutiny. Brands that operate transparently give critics less to invent and give AI systems more to work with. When an agent summarizes what you stand for, you want it drawing from your own documented record—not filling gaps with inference.

The failure mode is among the most damaging in the Answer Economy. When AI systems encounter a gap between a brand's public claims and third-party evidence, they hedge. "The company asserts . . ." or "According to the manufacturer . . ." are phrases that signal to the reader—human or machine—that the claim has not been independently verified. Accumulated hedging destroys credibility more quietly and more thoroughly than a single crisis.

## Clarify: Turn Complexity into Confidence

People are not bored by complexity. They are bored by bad explanations.

Parents worried about infant nutrition will read long, careful breakdowns if the language respects their intelligence. Consumers concerned about microplastics will engage deeply if the explanation is coherent.

In AI answers, the same pattern holds. The most appreciated responses are not the shortest, but the ones that organize confusion into a few understandable ideas.

Brands that clarify accept that their categories are complicated—and that explanation is part of the value exchange. They invest in organizing information, defining boundaries, and situating themselves honestly within the competitive landscape.

They also recognize that clarification is not just for humans. Structured, consistent explanations help models generate safer, more accurate answers that align with how the brand would explain things itself.[7] Structured schema markup—code embedded in webpages that labels key information such as product type, ingredients, reviews, or FAQs—helps search engines and AI systems interpret a page accurately. Pages using structured schema markup have shown nearly 60 percent higher visibility in AI-generated search results compared to pages without it. Clarity is not just good communication practice. It is machine legibility.

Clarification is generosity. It says, "We've done the work, so you don't have to."

The risk is predictable. Brands that hide behind complexity—technical jargon, regulatory boilerplate, deliberately ambiguous language—find that AI fills the clarity gap for them, often with less nuance and less favorable framing than the brand would have chosen. Agents trained on third-party simplification of your category will use that simplification, not yours. Cede the clarity, and you cede the narrative.

## Host: Stay Present in the Hard Conversations

Hosting means taking responsibility for the quality of the dialogue that surrounds your brand—not controlling it but showing up for it. It is the discipline most brands resist—and often the behavior that matters most.

PlanetFeedback was, at its core, a hosting experiment. It created a space where people could speak and companies could respond. Some companies treated responding to consumers on the platform as a nuisance. Others treated engaging with customers publicly as a responsibility.

At the Better Business Bureau, hosting took a more formal shape: structured dispute resolution, public accountability, and visible effort to resolve issues fairly. The process was not always comfortable—but the visible effort to respond to complaints and resolve disputes helped maintain public credibility.

In the Answer Economy, hosting means accepting that the conversation never really ends. It means showing up where your category is discussed, engaging without defensiveness and co-creating better answers with platforms and partners.

Hosting is not about control. That era is over. It's about responsibility for the quality of the dialogue you are part of.

This is why it's so urgently important for brand builders to build discipline around the "Ask Through." The relationship isn't over after the first question. In the Answer Economy, consumers drill down, and brands must be prepared for that exchange.

The failure mode is abandonment. Brands that go quiet when their categories are contested—that treat difficult questions as PR risks to be managed rather than conversations to be entered—create vacuums. Critics, competitors, and disgruntled customers fill those vacuums readily. An AI system trained on a category in which one brand has never participated in the dialogue will build its answers from everyone else's material.

## Ten Actions You Can Take Without Permission

Organizational transformation usually arrives wrapped in process: executive buy-in, budget cycles, roadmaps, and cross-functional alignment. But behavioral change rarely starts that way. It starts with evidence. With curiosity. With someone deciding to look more closely at how the world sees their brand.

If you finish this chapter on a Sunday night and feel the gap between the insight and action, here's the good news: You don't need permission to begin behaving differently. You can start Monday morning.

The actions below are reconnaissance missions. The purpose is to surface reality, quantify risk, and build a defensive case for why LATCH is not theoretical, but necessary. You don't need to do all of them. Do a few well. Document what you learn. Patterns will emerge.

### *Action 1: Test Your Answer Visibility (30 minutes)*

Ask at least three AI assistants the same five questions customers would plausibly ask in your category:

1. "What's the best [product type] for [specific use case]?"
2. "Is [your brand] worth the extra cost compared to [competitor]?"
3. "What should I know before buying [your category]?"
4. "What are common problems or risks with [your product type]?"
5. "Who shouldn't use [your product]?"

Document exactly where you appear, how you're framed, and what language is used. Note what evidence is cited—and what isn't.

This is not a vanity exercise. It's your baseline. You can't manage what you haven't seen.

### *Action 2: Audit Your Top 20 FAQs (45 minutes)*

Pull together four lists:

1. Your top twenty customer support tickets
2. Your top twenty organic search queries
3. Your top twenty negative product reviews
4. Your top twenty Reddit, forum, or community questions

Now compare those lists to your website's FAQ section. Count how many real customer questions your FAQs actually answer.

Most FAQs reveal a quiet truth: They are optimized for internal comfort, not external curiosity. This gap between the questions consumers actually ask and the questions your FAQ currently answers is **Answer Debt**.

### *Action 3: Search Your Own Risk Surface (20 minutes)*

Run these searches exactly as written:

- "[Your brand] safety concerns"
- "[Your brand] recall"
- "[Your brand] lawsuit"
- "[Your brand] ingredients"
- "[Your brand] controversy"
- Read the first page carefully.

Anything you didn't know? Anything you couldn't explain clearly to a friend? Anything outdated, misleading, or unresolved?

AI systems already see this material. If you can't contextualize it, they will—often without nuance.

### *Action 4: Check What Machines Can Actually Read (15 minutes)*

Open the source code of your primary product pages and look for structured data (schema.org or JSON-LD). If it exists, ask:

- Is it complete?
- Is it accurate?
- Is it current?

If it doesn't exist, understand the implication: Machines struggle to understand you.

Run the page through Google's Rich Results Test or similar tools. Checking whether machines can interpret your pages correctly is not just SEO trivia. It determines whether AI systems can understand and surface your content.

### *Action 5: Calculate Your Answer Debt (1 hour)*

Pull the last ninety days of customer service tickets and categorize them by question type:

- How do I use this?
- Is this safe for [condition] or [age group]?

- How does this compare to [alternative]?
- What happens if [edge case]?
- How do I return, troubleshoot, or maintain this?

Any question asked more than five times is answer debt—you owe an answer that hasn't been published clearly enough.

Now calculate the cost:

$$(\text{Number of tickets}) \times (\text{Average handling cost})$$

That dollar figure is the price of not answering well.

### *Action 6: Map Your Verification Gaps (30 minutes)*

List your top ten product or brand claims. For each, ask:

- Who verified this? (Internal? Third party? Nobody?)
- Where is that verification documented?
- Can someone outside the company access it?

Would an AI system treat this claim as a verified fact or hedge it as "according to the company"?

Count how many claims are externally verifiable. That number is your *verification readiness score.*

### *Action 7: Benchmark One Competitor (45 minutes)*

Choose your most credible competitor and run the same five AI Visibility questions from Action 1 above. Compare:

- Where they appear and you don't
- How they are described versus you
- What evidence is cited for them that isn't cited for you
- What questions they answer directly that you dodge

If they're ahead, reverse-engineer why. If they're behind, quantify your lead. Either way, you now have a concrete comparison, not an opinion.

### *Action 8: Create One Real Answer Page (2 hours)*

Pick the single most common customer question in your category. Write a page of roughly 500 words that:

- Answers the question clearly in the first paragraph
- Provides evidence and sources
- Addresses obvious follow-up questions
- Uses plain language, not marketing spin
- Includes basic structured data

Publish it. Share it internally. Track where it gets referenced.

One excellent answer changes the conversation faster than ten campaigns.

### *Action 9: Start a "Questions We Can't Answer" Log (Ongoing)*

Create a shared document. Anytime someone encounters a question they can't answer confidently, log it:

- What was asked?
- Why couldn't we answer it?
- What would we need to answer it well?

Review monthly. Prioritize recurring themes.

This log becomes your future roadmap, your risk register, and your case for investment.

### *Action 10: Build a Coalition, Not a Pitch (45 minutes)*

Share this chapter—or your findings from the actions above—with three people:

- A finance partner (frame as risk and cost)
- A customer service leader (frame as volume and clarity)
- A product or R&D lead (frame as differentiation and truth)

Ask one question: "What would it take to pilot this in one area?"

Transformation doesn't start with alignment. It starts with allies.

Complete three of these actions this week. Do six by month-end. Do all ten by quarter-end. By then, you won't be asking whether the Answer Economy maters. You'll be proving it does.

## Who Owns LATCH?

The question "Who owns LATCH?" will surface in the first meeting where you present the LATCH framework, and it deserves a direct answer.

LATCH is not a marketing initiative. It is not a communications program. It is not a technology implementation. It is an operating posture that cuts across every function that generates customer-facing signals, and in a modern organization, that is almost every function.

*Listen* lives closest to customer research, social intelligence, and customer service. *Answer* belongs to content, product marketing, and customer experience. *Tell the Truth* is shared between legal, communications, and brand, and it requires those three functions to actually coordinate, which many organizations have spent years avoiding. *Clarify* touches product design, regulatory affairs, and education. *Host* is the senior leadership responsibility because presence in a difficult conversation requires organizational authority to back it up.

The practice implication is that LATCH requires cross-functional leadership and ownership from someone with enough organizational standing to hold each function accountable for its piece of the behavioral record. In some companies, that is the Chief Marketing Officer (CMO). In others, it's the Chief Trust Officer, the Chief Experience Officer, or the Chief Digital Officer (my former role at Nestlé). In smaller organization, it is often the person who has the presence of mind to act.

The important thing is not the title. It is the commitment—that somewhere in the organization, someone is asking, regularly, whether the brand is truly latching onto LATCH, or merely claiming to.

## The Choice Ahead

The Answer Economy does not ask whether brands want to behave differently. It observes whether they do.

LATCH is not a framework for looking smarter to machines. It is a test of character under conditions of radical transparency. If you practice these behaviors consistently, something unexpected happens: The Answer Economy becomes less frightening. Agents can stop feeling like black boxes and start acting like mirrors, and you can apply the behaviors you already believe in.

LATCH connects to the measurement systems introduced earlier in this book. The VVR framework—Visibility, Vulnerability, and Readiness—measures the state of your brand's AI presence at a point in time. LATCH describes the behaviors that move these scores in the right direction. Visibility improves when you Listen and Answer. Vulnerability shrinks when you Tell the Truth and Clarify. Readiness grows when you Host your own narrative rather than cede it. The two frameworks are not parallel; they are sequential. LATCH is what you do. VVR is how you know whether it's working.

## Key Takeaways

- LATCH works only as a discipline, not a checklist—the behaviors must be practiced consistently across the organization, not checked off by a campaign team and forgotten.
- The behaviors are sequential and cumulative. Listening is the precondition for Answering well, Honesty is the precondition for Clarity, and Hosting without the first four behaviors is just theater.
- The window to shape what AI says about your brand is open now and narrowing. AI systems are already developing habits about which sources they trust. Brands that establish consistent behavioral records early hold a structural advantage that compounds over time.
- Honest, verifiable claims build more durable AI visibility than polished messaging. When AI systems encounter a gap between a brand's public claim and third-party evidence, they hedge. Accumulated hedging destroys credibility more than any single crisis.
- LATCH needs an organizational owner—someone with standing to hold every function accountable for its piece of the behavioral record. The framework will not survive as a marketing initiative. It requires cross-functional commitment and a regular cadence of honest assessment.

- The strongest long-term advantage is simple: consistently showing up with useful, honest answers. Tools, campaigns, and optimization frameworks will continue to change. The habit of showing up usefully, honestly, and consistently—in every conversation, human or machine mediated—is the one investment that does not depreciate.

# 8 The Six As of Answer Readiness

## Prompted Moment

*When someone asks a real question about your product—whether to a friend, a salesperson, a search engine, or an AI assistant—how well prepared is your brand to answer?*

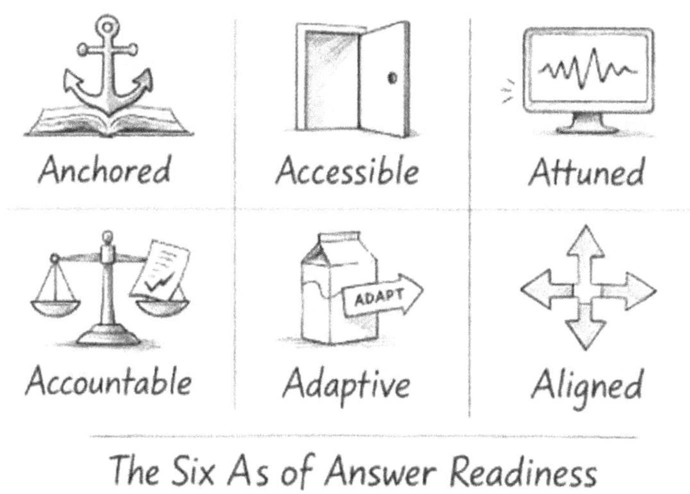

For most of modern marketing history, brands focused on messaging. The job was to project a story clearly and repeatedly enough that it shaped perception. Advertising, packaging, PR, and digital campaigns worked together to reinforce a brand narrative. The assumption was simple: If brands spoke loudly and consistently enough, consumers would listen.

The Answer Economy changes that dynamic. Consumers now begin with questions. They ask questions mid-task, mid-purchase, and mid-conversation: Is this product safe? Is it worth the price? What's better than this? What should I know before buying?

Increasingly, those questions are answered by AI systems that synthesize information from many sources: brand websites, reviews, regulators, journalists, retailers, and public data. In this environment, brands are judged not only by what they say. They are judged by how clearly and credibly they can answer questions when those questions appear.

This capability is what we call **Answer Readiness**. Answer Readiness is simple in principle: When someone asks a real question about your category, can your brand be explained clearly, credibly, and consistently? Brands that achieve this become easier for AI systems—and humans—to recommend. Brands that do not become harder to justify.

Consider a simple moment: A shopper in a grocery aisle asks their phone, "Is oat milk healthier than dairy milk?" The assistant scans articles, reviews, nutrition databases, and brand websites before responding. If the brand has clear explanations and evidence, the assistant answers confidently. If the information is vague or contradictory, the assistant hesitates—or recommends another product. That difference is Answer Readiness.

A useful rule of thumb is simple: If a brand welcomes questions the way systems like ChatGPT do—openly, directly, and without defensiveness—it likely demonstrates high Answer Readiness.

To make this capability operational, organizations must develop a set of practical disciplines. Answer Readiness becomes operational through six interdependent capabilities. Each capability addresses a common failure mode observed when brands are represented by AI systems. Together, these capabilities determine whether a brand can be trusted under scrutiny:

- **Anchored**—Stable, authoritative source of truth
- **Accessible**—Answers available where questions arise

- **Attuned**—Deep understanding of real consumer questions
- **Accountable**—Evidence-backed claims with clear ownership
- **Adaptive**—Capacity to update answers as conditions change
- **Aligned**—Consistent external expression across the organization

These six capabilities describe whether a brand can respond clearly when questions arise. Anchored organizations maintain a reliable source of truth explaining their products, policies, and claims. Accessible organizations ensure answers appear wherever confusion occurs—on websites, in search results, and through AI assistants. Attuned organizations understand the real questions people ask before making decisions. Accountable organizations support their claims with evidence that others can verify. Adaptive organizations update answers as products, research, or regulations change. Aligned organizations ensure that every team—from marketing to customer support—explains the brand in the same way.

## Anchored: Creating a Place for Answers to Stand

*Anchoring* describes whether a brand has a clearly defined source of truth that governs how products, policies, and claims are explained. Anchoring works because it transforms brand messaging into durable evidence. AI systems search for anchors when reconciling conflicting information. When no authoritative source exists—or when multiple versions compete—systems hedge, and hedging weakens recommendations.

Patagonia illustrates what strong anchoring looks like in practice. Patagonia's repair and care guides are unusually detailed. Rather than simply encouraging consumers to buy new products, Patagonia publishes extensive instructions explaining how to maintain and repair existing gear.[1]

When people ask whether Patagonia products last longer, AI systems can point to documented repair practices rather than vague marketing claims.

Patagonia's supply chain disclosures provide another anchor. The company publishes detailed factory lists, audit outcomes, and corrective actions for suppliers around the world. This documentation allows journalists, regulators, and AI systems alike to verify the brand's claims about responsible manufacturing.

Patagonia's Worn Wear program adds another layer. Through repair services and resale initiatives, Patagonia demonstrates durability in action.

Millions of repair interactions feed both product improvements and public storytelling.[2]

Patagonia does not ask consumers to simply trust its claims. It provides documentation that allows others to verify them.

Microsoft offers an example of anchoring in a very different category. When companies evaluate cloud services or AI systems, they ask questions about security, safety, and governance. Microsoft addresses these questions by publishing extensive transparency documentation.

Microsoft's Responsible AI Reports and Transparency Notes explain how its AI systems work, what their limitations are, and how risks are mitigated. These documents follow consistent formats so that both humans and machines can easily navigate them.[3]

When enterprises ask agents about Microsoft's AI safety practices, bias mitigation, or model limitations, responses cite specific sections from authoritative documentation rather than general claims. The anchoring creates confidence not through marketing language, but through verifiable, structured transparency.

Microsoft's result is like Patagonia's, even though the industries are very different. In both cases, the organization has created a reliable place where answers can stand.

## Accessible: Meeting Questions Where They Occur

Even the best documentation has limited value if people cannot find it. *Accessibility* means answers appear exactly when and where confusion occurs.

Canon provides a strong example. Photography is a technically complex category. Consumers frequently worry about compatibility between cameras, lenses, flashes, and accessories. They also struggle with settings and configuration.

Canon addresses these concerns through practical guides that answer specific questions. Instead of simply listing product specifications, Canon publishes scenario-based tutorials: how to shoot sports photography, how to capture images in low light, how to configure autofocus for moving subjects.[4] These guides are often tied to specific camera models, which allows both consumers and AI systems to retrieve precise answers.

Canon also maintains a lens compatibility database that allows users to check whether lenses and cameras purchased years apart will work together. For photographers building equipment over time, this question appears constantly. By publishing compatibility data in a searchable format, Canon prevents guesswork.

Accessibility turns complex products into confident decisions. Accessibility matters because most questions occur in moments of uncertainty. A photographer adjusting settings in the field, a shopper comparing products in a store aisle, or a technician troubleshooting equipment rarely has time to read lengthy documentation. Clear answers must appear immediately. When brands organize information so it can be easily retrieved by search engines, AI assistants, and humans alike, they remove friction from the decision process.

## Attuned: Listening Before Explaining

Many brands organize their communication around what they want to say. *Attuned* brands organize around what people want to know. This distinction becomes obvious when examining real consumer questions.

Across categories, the same questions appear repeatedly: Is this safe? Is it worth the price? What are the downsides? How does it compare to alternatives?

Brands that anticipate these questions reduce confusion early. These questions rarely originate in marketing departments. They emerge from search queries, customer service logs, product reviews, and conversations with retailers. When companies analyze these signals carefully, patterns appear. The same uncertainties surface repeatedly. Attuned organizations treat these questions as strategic intelligence rather than inconvenience.

Oatly produces oat-based milk alternatives used as substitutes for dairy milk in a category filled with debate. Consumers often ask questions about nutrition, ingredients, environmental impact, and processing methods. Rather than avoiding these topics, Oatly addresses them directly. Its FAQ pages and packaging answer questions about sugar levels, ingredient sourcing, environmental impact, and suitability for different diets.[5]

Oatly's explanations often include nuance. Instead of claiming oat milk is universally healthier than dairy, the company explains trade-offs between categories and consumption contexts. This approach reduces skepticism because it mirrors the questions consumers already have.

Attuned brands listen first and explain second.

## Accountable: Standing Behind What You Say

In the Answer Economy, credibility depends on evidence. AI systems consistently rely on sources that demonstrate verification—regulators, academic institutions, independent testing organizations, and reputable publications. When brand claims lack evidence, AI systems often introduce caveats. *Accountability* means organizations support their claims with documentation that others can verify.

Patagonia's supply-chain disclosures, Canon's repair commitments, and government-backed health institutions like the UK's National Health Service (NHS) demonstrate this principle.

The NHS publishes extensive health guidance covering symptoms, treatments, and prevention strategies. These pages include citations to medical research and are maintained by clinical experts. Because the information is clearly sourced and regularly reviewed, AI systems frequently cite NHS content when answering health-related questions.

AI systems tend to rely more heavily on sources that demonstrate verification. Medical institutions, regulators, independent laboratories, and academic research are typically treated as more reliable than marketing claims alone. Brands that publish supporting evidence—such as certifications, testing results, or third-party evaluations—therefore become easier for AI systems to cite with confidence.

Accountability transforms answers from opinion into evidence. For consumers, this builds trust. For machines, it reduces uncertainty.

## Adaptive: Updating Truth as the World Changes

Information ages quickly. Scientific knowledge evolves. Regulations change. Products improve. New risks emerge. In fast-moving categories such as health, finance, or technology, outdated answers can spread quickly if organizations fail to update their information. Brands that fail to update their answers accumulate contradictions. *Adaptive* organizations update information continuously.

The UK's National Health Service again provides a strong example. Medical guidance on symptoms, treatments, and public health advice is revised regularly as research evolves. During the COVID-19 pandemic, NHS guidance changed frequently as scientists learned more about the virus.[6] Because these updates propagate quickly across NHS websites and apps, AI systems often rely on NHS pages when answering health questions.

Adaptation ensures that answers remain credible over time. Without it, outdated explanations quietly erode trust.

## Aligned: Speaking with One Voice

Even accurate information can become confusing if different teams explain it differently.

*Alignment* means marketing, legal, product teams, and customer service describe products and policies consistently.

Misalignment often appears in subtle ways: marketing benefits that customer service cannot confirm, product documentation that contradicts advertising claims, and legal disclaimers that undermine marketing language. AI systems surface these inconsistencies immediately.

When sources conflict, answers become cautious and uncertain. Alignment requires coordination across the organization. It rarely happens automatically.

But when alignment is strong, AI systems can synthesize brand information confidently.

## How the Six As Show Up in Practice

Table 8.1 illustrates how selected organizations perform across the six dimensions of Answer Readiness: Anchored, Accessible, Attuned, Accountable, Adaptive, and Aligned. The scores are not intended as precise measurement. Rather, they provide an illustrative view of how Answer Readiness becomes visible in real organizations.

Several patterns emerge. Organizations that perform strongly across the six dimensions rarely treat answers as a marketing function alone. Instead, they treat documentation, transparency, and customer questions as part of their operational infrastructure. Product teams, support teams, and governance processes all contribute to ensuring that claims remain clear, verifiable, and consistent.

**Table 8.1 The 6 As in Practice: Readiness Levels by Brand**

| Organization | Anchored | Accessible | Attuned | Accountable | Adaptive | Aligned | Total |
|---|---|---|---|---|---|---|---|
| Patagonia | High | Medium | Medium | High | Medium | High | High |
| Apple | High | High | Low | Medium | High | High | High |
| Fairphone | High | Medium | Medium | High | Medium | Medium | High |
| REI | Low | High | High | Medium | Medium | Medium | Medium |
| Chewy | Medium | High | High | Low | Medium | Medium | High |
| Ikea | Medium | High | Medium | Low | Medium | Medium | Medium |
| Oatly | Low | Medium | High | Low | Medium | Medium | Low |

Readiness levels across the six "A" capabilities for selected brands, translated from numerical scores into qualitative levels (High, Medium, Low) to highlight comparative strengths in Answer Readiness.

Some organizations excel in only a few dimensions. Some publish extensive documentation but fail to make it easily discoverable. Others understand customer questions well but struggle to align answers across departments. The table highlights these imbalances and shows why Answer Readiness depends on coordination across the organization rather than strength in a single capability.

A few examples illustrate how these differences appear in practice for a number of brands:

- **REI:** REI scores strongly in the *Accessible* and *Attuned* dimensions. The outdoor retailer has invested heavily in educational resources that help customers navigate complex purchasing decisions. Gear guides, product comparisons, and skills tutorials answer practical questions about equipment selection and outdoor skills. These resources function as a knowledge infrastructure. When consumers search for questions such as how to choose a backpack or sleeping bag, REI's guides often appear prominently because they address real decisions clearly and directly.[7]
- **Apple:** Apple illustrates strong performance in the *Aligned* dimension. Product pages, support documentation, developer materials, and retail training consistently describe features and limitations using similar language. This consistency allows explanations to travel cleanly across websites, support forums, and AI-generated summaries. When users ask how Face ID works or how Apple's privacy protections function, explanations remain stable regardless of where the question appears.[8]
- **Stack Overflow:** Stack Overflow demonstrates strong *Attunement* because their knowledge bases originate from real user questions. Millions of developer questions have been organized into structured explanations that mirror the practical challenges programmers encounter daily.[9] Because the knowledge base evolves directly from real questions, the resulting answers align closely with real-world needs.
- **Wikipedia:** Wikipedia illustrates *Anchoring* through its structured approach to sourcing and editorial governance. Articles are built on verifiable references and include citations, revision histories, and

transparent editorial discussion pages. Because claims must be supported by reliable sources, readers—and automated systems—can trace information back to its origin. This transparency creates a stable knowledge anchor frequently consulted when explaining historical events, scientific concepts, or public figures.[10]

- **Consumer Reports:** Consumer Reports demonstrates *Accountability* through independent product testing. The nonprofit purchases products anonymously at retail and evaluates them through controlled laboratory tests using standardized methodologies. Results are published alongside clear explanations of testing criteria and performance comparisons. Because these evaluations are conducted independently from manufacturers, journalists, regulators, and technology systems often treat Consumer Reports as a credible verification source when comparing product performance.[11]
- **Netflix:** Netflix illustrates *Adaptive* capability through continuous updates to its platform and supporting documentation. The company regularly refines recommendation systems, streaming technologies, and user controls as viewing patterns and technologies evolve. Help resources and product guidance are updated alongside these changes so users searching for explanations—such as how recommendations work or how parental controls function—receive information reflecting the platform's latest features.[12]

## How the Six As Interact: Understanding Failure Modes

The six capabilities reinforce each other. Weakness in one area can undermine strength in another. Consider a few common failure patterns:

- A brand publishes extensive FAQ content but claims lack independent verification. AI systems may respond: "According to the brand, the product offers these benefits, though independent confirmation is limited." Visibility without credibility rarely produces strong recommendations.
- A company invests heavily in certifications and research but stores documentation in long PDF reports buried deep within corporate

websites. AI systems may overlook the evidence entirely. Credibility exists, but it remains invisible.
- An organization understands exactly which questions consumers ask, but different departments answer those questions inconsistently. AI systems detect conflicting information and hedge. Listening alone does not produce trust.

Most organizations do not fail across all six dimensions. More commonly, brands perform well in two or three areas and struggle in the others.

The strategic opportunity lies in identifying the weakest capabilities. Improving even one weak area—clarifying documentation, strengthening verification, or aligning explanations—can significantly improve how a brand appears in AI-generated answers.

Answer Readiness compounds quietly. Every clear answer reduces confusion. Every verified claim increases confidence. Over time these improvements accumulate. Each clear explanation becomes easier for search engines, retailers, journalists, and AI assistants to reuse. As answers circulate across platforms, the brand becomes easier to explain and easier to recommend.

Every aligned explanation strengthens credibility. In the Answer Economy, the brands that succeed will not necessarily be the loudest. They will be the ones most prepared to answer.

## Key Takeaways

- Anchored brands create a reliable source of truth. When documentation, product information, and policies are clearly organized and authoritative, both consumers and AI systems can explain the brand confidently and consistently.
- Accessible brands ensure answers appear where questions arise. When information is easy to find in search results, product pages, and support resources, uncertainty disappears and decisions become faster and more confident.
- Attuned brands organize communication around real customer questions. By studying search behavior, reviews, and customer service conversations, organizations learn what people genuinely want to know before making decisions.

- Accountable brands support claims with evidence others can verify. Independent research, certifications, testing results, and expert validation transform marketing promises into credible explanations that both humans and AI systems trust.
- Adaptive brands continuously update answers as conditions evolve. When research changes, products improve, or regulations shift, organizations must revise their explanations quickly to prevent outdated information from eroding credibility.
- Aligned brands communicate consistently across the entire organization. When marketing, product teams, legal, and customer service explain things the same way, brands become easier for people—and machines—to understand and recommend.

# 9 Crisis and Governance in the Answer Economy

## Prompted Moment

*How do you respond when the first signal of a crisis shows up inside an AI answer—not the news?*

It is 10:47 on a Sunday night. A woman sits at her kitchen table with a folder of paperwork in front of her. Tomorrow morning, she has an appointment to sign a debt consolidation agreement—one that will combine four credit cards into a single monthly payment she can afford. She has been working toward this for eight months.

Before she closes her laptop, she types one question into an AI assistant: "Is [company name] a legitimate debt consolidation company?"

The system does not find a definitive answer. It finds fragments. A Better Business Bureau complaint from 2023. A state attorney general investigation—opened, then quietly dropped. A Reddit thread where someone describes feeling pressured into fees they didn't expect. The AI synthesizes these into a careful, hedged response. It does not say the company is fraudulent. It says, "Some consumers have raised concerns."

She reads it twice. She closes the folder.

In the morning, she calls to cancel the appointment. She tells the representative she changed her mind. She does not mention the AI. The representative notes the cancellation and moves on.

No complaint was filed. No review was written. No one at the company knows a Sunday night query cost them a client—or that the attorney general investigation it surfaced was closed without findings, or that the Reddit thread described a different company entirely.

The answer was not wrong enough to flag. It was just uncertain enough to decide.

She does not write a review. She does not file a complaint. But three days later, her coworker mentions she is struggling with credit card debt. The woman shakes her head.

"I looked into one of those consolidation companies," she says. "The AI basically told me to stay away."

She doesn't remember the details. She just remembers the feeling—uncertain enough to decide—and that is what she passes on to her coworker. Her coworker doesn't look them up at all.

Brands that listen early still have time. Brands that listen late encounter their crisis the same way their customers do—through an answer they did not write.

## Brand Crisis in the Age of AI Answers

This chapter is about a new kind of crisis—one that does not begin with a headline, a recall notice, or a viral post. This kind of crisis begins with a question posed to an AI answer engine.

In the Answer Economy, AI systems now serve as the first point of contact between a concerned consumer and a brand's reputation.

Crisis management in the Answer Economy is an intelligence and governance function; it is no longer a communications function. The brands that understand this are the ones that survive.

AI answer engines are designed to reduce uncertainty for users, especially in high-stakes contexts involving health, safety, finances, or children. In those situations, the systems apply conservative logic. When evidence appears incomplete, inconsistent, or unresolved, the systems surface caution, fundamentally reshaping how crises begin.

A product recall, safety concern, or compliance issue no longer requires a triggering headline. A small number of consumers asking, "Is this safe?" or "Does this apply to me?" can initiate a cascade. If authoritative clarification is not immediately available, AI systems synthesize from secondary sources: regulatory databases, older articles, consumer forums, and activist commentary.

The resulting answer rarely sounds alarmist. It sounds careful. Phrases such as "concerns have been raised" or "evidence is mixed" introduce doubt without accusation. That doubt, however, influences behavior at scale.

In AI-mediated environments, uncertainty travels faster than reassurance.

### *When the Old Playbook Runs Out of Pages*

Search-era crisis management assumed choice. Consumers could click multiple links, compare viewpoints, and interpret context. Brands relied on that friction to slow escalation and buy time.

Answer engines eliminate friction. They synthesize across sources and deliver a single response. They do not invite exploration. They do not wait for clarification. When an answer engine states that "a product has been recalled" or that "safety concerns remain unresolved," the system rarely distinguishes between an active recall, a historical incident, or a resolved issue unless that distinction is clearly documented and machine legible.

Consequently, crises now feel sudden and disorienting. Internal approval cycles remain calibrated for press statements and regulatory filings. AI systems operate continuously. By the time internal teams align, the answer has already circulated across chat interfaces, screenshots, and agent-assisted shopping environments.

There is no page two in an answer.

Empirical browsing data supports the structural shift from active exploration to passive acceptance of a single synthesized answer. An analysis by the Pew Research Center found that when AI-generated summaries appeared in Google search results, users clicked traditional search links roughly half as often as they did when no AI summary was present. In many cases, users ended their browsing session entirely after reading the AI-generated answer, reinforcing how conversational interfaces compress exploration and concentrate authority in a single synthesized response.[1]

## Early Radar: Seeing Crisis While It Is Still Malleable

*Early radar* means monitoring questions, not just sentiment or coverage. In the Answer Economy, early radar is not a communications advantage. It is a survival capability.

Early radar tracks shifts in what people are asking, where reassurance is being sought, and which topics suddenly generate uncertainty. Call center transcripts, chatbot logs, warranty inquiries, and AI prompt analysis consistently surface crisis signals before any spike in social media or press attention.

Across BrandRank.AI's client engagements, the pattern is consistent. Consumers test concerns quietly before amplifying them publicly. They ask the same questions repeatedly, probing for safety, legality, or reassurance. When those questions go unanswered—or receive inconsistent responses—escalation follows.

Most organizations were never designed to listen this way. Marketing teams focus on persuasion. Communications teams focus on media. Legal teams focus on liability. Customer service teams focus on resolution. AI answers cut across all these functions and move faster than any one of them.

Early radar closes the gap between when a crisis enters the AI answer layer and when leadership can respond to it—treating questions as strategic signals rather than operational noise.

At Nestlé, we built the Digital Acceleration Team partly to address an early version of this challenge. From a centralized command center staffed by dozens of full-time monitors, we tracked brand health in real time—screens lit with social chatter, customer service inquiries, and emerging issues from across the globe. Signals surfaced early. Issues became visible before they escalated.[2]

That capability mattered. It still does. But in today's environment, it is no longer enough.

BrandRank.AI data suggests four question categories that consistently precede AI-mediated crises, often by weeks:

1. Safety and ingredient questions ("Is this safe for children?")
2. Recall and withdrawal questions ("Has this product been recalled?")
3. Comparison questions that invoke safety ("Is Brand X safer than Brand Y?")
4. Regulatory questions ("Has this product been approved by the FDA?")

Organizations that monitor these four categories continuously—across AI platforms, not just social media—close the gap between signal and response.[3]

Real-time monitoring without real-time decision authority, however, creates a dangerous illusion of control. Signals may be detected instantly—and still stall in organizational handoffs, legal reviews, and hierarchical approval loops while AI systems continue answering in the background. That's a governance problem—and it requires a governance solution.

The uncomfortable implication: Senior leadership can no longer be downstream from crisis intelligence. In AI-mediated crises, the decision to act must be wired directly into the signal layer—not filtered through weekly updates or department summaries. Speed now depends less on dashboards than on governance: who owns the answer, who can update authoritative sources, and who is empowered to act before uncertainty hardens.

## The AI-Era Crisis Checklist

Before a crisis spreads through AI answers, organizations should prepare several capabilities in advance. Traditional crisis communications plans focus on media response. In the Answer Economy, preparation also requires ensuring that AI systems encounter accurate, structured information when they synthesize answers.

Five preparations are especially critical:

1. **Monitor high-risk questions continuously.** Organizations should track how major AI systems answer safety, recall, regulatory, and comparison questions about their products. Early monitoring allows teams to detect emerging vulnerability before it spreads widely across answer engines.
2. **Maintain a structured crisis information hub.** Brands should maintain a centralized repository containing recall notices, product identifiers, safety guidance, and frequently asked questions in machine-readable formats. When a crisis occurs, this hub becomes the authoritative source AI systems draw from.
3. **Pre-approve answer frameworks for high-risk scenarios.** Issues such as ingredient safety, product recalls, regulatory warnings, and eligibility rules should have pre-reviewed response structures. These frameworks allow organizations to publish clear guidance quickly without waiting for prolonged approval cycles.
4. **Assign a cross-functional escalation owner.** Answer-level crises often move faster than traditional communications processes. A designated escalation leader should have authority to coordinate across legal, product, communications, and digital teams and publish clarifications rapidly.
5. **Stress-test answers before a crisis emerges.** Organizations should regularly test how AI systems respond to sensitive prompts about safety, reliability, and regulatory compliance. These tests reveal where documentation gaps or inconsistent language may later create answer vulnerability.

These steps do not eliminate risk. But they ensure that when AI systems synthesize information about a crisis, they are more likely to encounter structured guidance from the brand itself rather than fragmented speculation. Preparation does not prevent the crisis. It determines whether the brand controls the answer when it arrives.

## Brand Vulnerability as a Crisis Predictor

Brand vulnerability, as measured through VVR (Visibility, Vulnerability, and Readiness), is covered in depth in Chapter 6. In crisis conditions, it operates differently—not as a metric to monitor, but as a countdown to crisis exposure.

A brand carrying elevated vulnerability before a crisis event is structurally exposed.

When a triggering moment arrives—a recall notice, a regulatory action, a viral consumer complaint—the brand does not start from neutral ground. AI systems have already assembled a narrative pattern, and if that pattern includes hedged claims, unresolved contradictions, or thin documentation, the AI answer will amplify the uncertainty rather than contain it.

That difference in pre-crisis documentation separates brands that contain AI-era crises from those that lose control of them. The crisis does not create the vulnerability. The crisis reveals it—at speed, at scale, and without warning.

Tracking vulnerability at the question level requires moving from *brand monitoring*—which measures what people say—to *answer monitoring*, which measures what AI systems synthesize and serve. That distinction matters. A brand can have clean social sentiment and severe answer vulnerability at the same time.

One tool built specifically to track answer level vulnerability in real time is the BrandRank.AI dashboard, which dynamically interrogates brand claims (e.g. "all natural," "clinically proven") via the answer engines.[4]

Persistent disagreement between what the brand claims and what AI systems say is not neutral. It signals that the system lacks confidence in the brand's narrative and that lack of confidence will compound when a crisis arrives.

Disagreement often appears long before a crisis becomes visible. An answer engine may phrase concerns carefully—"some sources question," "evidence is mixed," "claims are not independently verified." Internally, these phrases may seem minor. To consumers, they introduce doubt. To retailers and platforms, they introduce risk.

When vulnerability is high, every new question becomes more dangerous. Each additional inquiry gives the system another opportunity to surface unresolved contradictions. Over time, those contradictions harden into narrative defaults.

The most common sources of vulnerability include outdated claims, inconsistent language across brand properties, missing evidence for premium assertions, and unresolved historical issues that remain computationally visible. In many cases, the brand believes the issue has been addressed when the answer engine does not.

Traditional *sentiment tracking* monitors how people feel about a brand after content has been published and consumed. It measures the emotional register of public conversation. Vulnerability tracking operates upstream of that signal—it measures whether the underlying source material AI systems draw from is reliable, consistent, and favorable before that material becomes a crisis.

## Recalls as a Crisis Stress Test for Answer Readiness

Product recalls reveal the new crisis dynamics with clarity. Historically, recall effectiveness depended on press coverage, retailer compliance, and consumer outreach. Today, recall effectiveness depends on how quickly authoritative information becomes usable by AI systems.

In cases where brands respond quickly—publishing clear product lists, step-by-step consumer guidance, and straightforward safety information in formats AI systems can read—AI answers shift toward accuracy within hours. Brands that delay, or publish information only through press releases and legal statements, see AI answers remain uncertain for days. In these cases, AI systems continue to surface cautionary language because no single authoritative source resolves the uncertainty. Retailer agents and shopping assistants respond accordingly, deprioritizing affected products and, in some cases, substituting alternatives automatically.

In a recall, the AI answer is not a side effect of the crisis. It is the crisis.

## When AI Amplifies What Brands Leave Unresolved

Public discussion often frames AI crisis risk as a hallucination problem. For large, established brands, hallucinations are relatively rare.

Hallucinations—the tendency of AI systems to generate plausible-sounding but fabricated content—are real, but rare for established brands with substantial digital footprints. What is far more common is **amplification**: the surfacing of legitimate but unfavorable content that would otherwise stay buried in search results, forum threads, and regulatory archives.

AI systems are exceptionally good at surfacing unresolved issues. Old controversies, partial truths, outdated claims, and inconsistent documentation remain computationally visible. If resolution is not clearly documented and easy to retrieve, the system treats the issue as open.

From the system's perspective, unresolved criticism signals risk. Silence or inconsistency reinforces that signal. The AI does not invent the problem. The AI magnifies it.

This dynamic is not new—only the speed and scale are. Long before AI answer engines existed, dissatisfaction spread asymmetrically. When I wrote *Satisfied Customer Tells Three Friends, Angry Customers Tell 3,000*, the lesson was not about marketing. It was about human behavior. People shared delight collectively. They shared frustration urgently. And they share unresolved frustration relentlessly.

AI has not changed that dynamic; it has mechanized it. The multiplier effect that once depended on social networks now operates at system speed. What once took months of accumulation can now surface in days and sometimes even hours.

Independent research examining how AI assistants summarize news content points to a similar pattern. A large international study coordinated by the European Broadcasting Union found that nearly half of tested AI responses contained significant issues, with the most common problems arising not from hallucinations but from sourcing, context, and synthesis errors. In other words, many misleading outputs originated in real underlying material that was incomplete, outdated, or poorly integrated rather than fabricated entirely by the model.[5]

This dynamic explains why crises often feel unfair to leadership. Internally, the issue was addressed years ago. Externally, the evidence still appears mixed.

In the Answer Economy, resolution must be legible, current, and structured.

## When Crisis Arrives: Taking Control of the Answer

When leaders first encounter a negative AI response, the instinct is defensive: Why is the model saying this? Where is this coming from? Is this misinformation?

Those reactions are understandable—and often misplaced.

AI answers are not opinions. They are syntheses. Every expression of caution, qualification, or doubt is anchored in underlying sources: regulatory databases, legacy media coverage, consumer forums, return logs, activist content, academic research, and brand-owned material.

The critical question is not whether the answer is negative. The critical question is:

*Which sources are influencing the answer?*

Without analytical visibility into those sources, brands argue with the output instead of correcting the inputs. Responses become reactive. Explanations become defensive. And the system continues to surface the same uncertainty because nothing upstream has changed.

Modern crisis management therefore requires a new discipline: *source-level diagnosis*. When brands can trace negative impressions back to their origin—an outdated claim, an unresolved safety clarification, a historical incident still computationally visible—they regain control. Fix the source, and the answer follows. Ignore the source, and the answer hardens. The mechanics of an AI-era crisis are now clear, but they don't explain why the same failure repeats itself, across, industries, at scale. The reason is not algorithmic. It is organizational. Most brands are not vulnerable because AI systems are unpredictable; they are vulnerable because no one inside the organization is responsible for what these systems say, before, during, or after a crisis arrives. The absence is not a gap in technology; it's a gap in governance.

## The Governance Gap: Who Owns the Answer?

The analysis above explains how AI-era crises propagate. What it does not yet explain is why most brands remain structurally vulnerable to AI crises—not once, but repeatedly, across categories, across years, regardless of how experienced their communications teams are. The answer is not a messaging failure. It is a governance failure. In most organizations, the problem lives simultaneously across six functions—Digital and Communications, Search and SEO, Corporate Affairs, Customer Service, Legal and Compliance, and Product and R&D—and no single function owns the synthesis.

The most common source of AI vulnerability is not a crisis event. It is ordinary inconsistency—the kind that accumulates quietly across functions until a consumer or customer ask a simple question and AI cannot give a straight answer.

A personal-care brand offers a clean illustration of how this happens. The brand labeled a product "fragrance-free" on its packaging, "unscented" on its website, and "lightly fragranced" in customer support scripts. The formula was unchanged across all three. No deception was intended. The product team documented ingredients in technical nomenclature. Marketing translated ingredient language into consumer-friendly claims without shared definitions. Regulatory disclosures listed processing aids that marketing materials omitted. Customer service scripts used conditional language to manage complaints.

When a consumer asked an AI assistant whether the product was safe for sensitive skin, the answer varied depending on which surface the agent happened to weight most. Sometimes it said "generally safe." Sometimes it said "some fragrance-sensitive users have reported reactions." Sometimes it introduced a caveat about processing aids. Marketing could not resolve the inconsistency of the responses. Legal could not resolve it. Customer service could not resolve it.

This is not unusual. It is the norm.

A national consumer bank offers a second illustration. Its marketing emphasized "easy banking, no surprises." When consumers asked AI assistants whether the bank charged fees, agent answers became qualified. Responses cited overdraft exceptions, conditional service charges, and policy variations depending on account type. Agent language relied on phrases such as "generally," "in some cases," and "depending on usage." The bank did not engage in deceptive practices. Fee disclosures lived in account agreements. Marketing summaries simplified the language. Customer service scripts described edge cases. Policy updates propagated unevenly. No one owned the reconciliation.

What both cases share is not bad intent. What they share is the absence of a single owner of product truth—someone empowered to resolve contradictions between functions before they harden into AI vulnerability.

In 2024, that absence became a legal question as well as a strategic one. In *Moffatt v. Air Canada*, the British Columbia Civil Resolution Tribunal held Air Canada responsible for incorrect guidance provided by its AI chatbot—regardless of whether the organization had authored the misstatement.[6] The legal precedent established that brands are accountable for what automated systems say on their behalf. Answer governance is no longer just about reputation. It is about legal exposure.

## Who Governs the Answer?

If governance is the answer, the next question is obvious: Who governs? Again, in most organizations, this question lives simultaneously across six functions, and no single function owns the synthesis. The consequences of that reality tend to play out the same way across functions:

- **Digital and Communications.** Digital and communications teams understand brand narrative, own the content calendar, and are accountable for how the brand appears in earned and owned media. Answer Readiness looks, on the surface, like an extension of brand presence work. The problem is that communications teams are optimized for human readers: tone, narrative arc, persuasion. AI agents do not respond to tone. They respond to consistency, evidence, and structure. A beautifully written brand story that contradicts a product specification creates more vulnerability than no story at all. Communications teams, working in isolation, cannot reconcile what lives in the product documentation layer.

- **Search and SEO.** SEO teams already think about how machines interpret brand content. They understand structured data, schema markup, and the logic of algorithmic ranking. The transition from "How does Google read this?" to "How does an AI agent read this?" is shorter for SEO than for any other function in the organization. But SEO was built for a world of documents and links. Answer agents synthesize across structured and unstructured sources, simultaneously including customer service transcripts, policy language, employee forums, and third-party databases that SEO has never touched. SEO authority does not translate to answer authority.

  In BrandRank.AI audits, several brands with dominant page-one search rankings still received qualified AI answers because agents synthesized information from regulatory filings, product reviews, and consumer forums—sources outside traditional SEO optimization.
- **Corporate Affairs.** Corporate communications owns the relationship with regulators, media, and institutional audiences. When an AI-era crisis surfaces, corporate communications has the most established crisis-response infrastructure: playbooks, spokespeople, legal liaisons, escalation protocols. The problem is that corporate communications is reactive by design. It responds to events. Answer Readiness requires continuous, pre-crisis ownership of how the brand is documented across every surface an agent might access. No corporate communications team is staffed to audit product pages, customer service scripts, and technical documentation on a rolling basis.
- **Customer Service.** Customer service teams are closer to actual consumer questions than any other function. They sit on the

transcripts, the call logs, the chatbot interactions—which are now primary source material for AI agents synthesizing brand answers. But customer service is optimized for resolution of individual interactions, not governance of brand-wide truth. Representatives are trained to de-escalate, not to ensure that every answer they give is consistent with what the marketing team published this week. The scale of the function—thousands of representatives, millions of interactions—makes coordination with other functions structurally difficult.

- **Product and R&D.** Product and R&D teams own the underlying truth. They know what the product contains, what its limitations are, and what claims can be substantiated. If any function should anchor brand documentation, it is the function that built the product. But product teams communicate in technical language designed for engineers and regulators, not for consumers or AI agents. R&D documentation is often proprietary, siloed, and written with a precision that makes it inaccessible to synthesis. Product truth and consumer-facing truth frequently diverge—and no one in the product team is accountable for that gap.
- **Legal and Compliance.** Post-*Moffatt*, legal teams have a direct liability interest in ensuring AI systems do not misrepresent the brand. Legal and compliance own the disclosure language, the regulatory filings, and the authoritative record of what the brand has formally committed to. But legal optimizes for precision and limitation—hedging language that protects against liability. AI agents interpret hedged language as uncertainty and respond conservatively. A legal team that rewrites all brand claims to be maximally defensive will produce a brand that sounds permanently untrustworthy to every AI system that encounters it.

The pattern is consistent across: Each has part of the answer; none has all of it. Answer Readiness fails at the seams—where marketing's language diverges from the product's documentation, where customer service scripts contradict legal disclosures. The governance question is not "Which function?" It is "Who coordinates across all of them, with the authority to resolve contradictions before a crisis makes them visible?"

In many organizations, this responsibility most naturally sits within Corporate Affairs or a central trust function. Communications teams already coordinate across legal, marketing, product, and customer service during crises and operate close to senior leadership when reputational risk emerges. In the Answer Economy, that coordination must evolve from episodic crisis management to continuous answer stewardship.

AI systems do not experience organizations the way employees do. They do not see departments, reporting lines, or approval processes. Instead, they evaluate evidence across the entire enterprise at once—product specifications, legal disclosures, customer service transcripts, regulatory filings, employee commentary, and third-party discussion. In doing so, they expose contradictions that traditional organizational structures were designed to tolerate. AI does not care about org charts—but it exposes them.

### *The Role Employees Play in Crisis Vulnerability*

Before we cover what good governance looks like, we need to address a crisis vulnerability that most organizations have not yet confronted—one that lives inside the organization itself: the organization's employees. Employees already contribute to the corpus AI agents draw from when they answer questions about your brand, and most have no idea their words are becoming source material for these AI agents.

Customer service transcripts. LinkedIn posts and conversations. Technical support tickets. Product manager documentation. Sales call notes. Social media posts. Forum responses. Slack conversations that leak into public channels. All of these become source material that AI agents can access, synthesize, and cite when answering questions about your brand.

The frontline employee who answers a frustrated customer on Reddit isn't just solving one person's problem. They're creating a data point that may be referenced thousands of times in AI-generated answers. The product manager who writes "this feature is buggy but we're working on it" in a GitHub issue isn't just communicating with developers—they're potentially feeding future AI characterizations of your product quality.

The fact that every employee interaction is potentially source material fundamentally changes the stakes for several organizational functions. Customer service representatives need to understand they are speaking to future training sets, not just current customers. Their language, tone, accuracy, and transparency don't just affect one interaction—they become part of the corpus AI systems draw from. A representative who hedges, contradicts official guidance, or fails to document resolutions can create vulnerability that persists long after the original issue is resolved.

Product managers can no longer treat internal documentation as internal. Technical specifications, known issues, limitation descriptions, and roadmap discussions increasingly leak into spaces AI systems can access—through community forums, support tickets, or user-generated content that references internal language. When employees post about workplace conditions, company policies, or product experiences, those posts become brand reputation signals. An engineer expressing frustration about quality control on social media or a former employee posting on Glassdoor about ethics concerns—these are not just HR issues. They are Answer Economy vulnerabilities that agents may cite when consumers ask about your brand's trustworthiness.

But here is what the governance conversation often misses: The same logic that makes employees a vulnerability makes them a structural asset when the internal reality genuinely matches the external claim.

Costco demonstrates what happens when employee experience becomes a visible brand asset. Costco's employee compensation, retention rates, and workplace satisfaction are extensively documented—not just by the company, but by current and former employees across multiple platforms. When consumers ask agents "Is Costco ethical?" or "Does Costco treat workers fairly?" agents can cite verifiable employee testimony, compensation data, and third-party verification.

When internal reality matches external claims, the reinforcing loop works in the brand's favor. Authentic employee experience generates signals that AI systems find consistently credible and easy to use. Conversely, contradictory signals between what the brand claims and what employees actually experience are exactly the kind of unresolved inconsistency AI systems are built to detect; any contradictions will hurt the brand.

Conflicting sustainability claims are illustrative of the harm that a brand can suffer when bold commitments posted for employees contradict hedged language and consumer-facing materials. Answer engines don't resolve the inconsistency in the brand's favor. They surface it. The result is what might be called *AI cynicism*—a pattern where the system learns to treat a brand sustainability narrative as unreliable because the signals don't agree with each other.

The message for leadership is not to control what your employees say. That instinct will fail, and the inauthenticity it produces makes the vulnerability worse. The message should be to ensure that internal reality matches the external claim. When it does, employees become the distributed documentation layer that stabilizes AI answers before any crisis begins.

Employee social media policies were designed for a world where reputation moved at human speed. In the Answer Economy, the stakes are permanent, searchable, and synthesizable. Organizations that govern this reality will maintain answer coherence. Organizations that ignore it will discover they have outsourced brand representation to whoever happened to be working the phones when a frustrated customer asked a hard question.

### *The Role Bots Play in Crisis Vulnerability*

Employee governance, for all its difficulty, is at least grounded in identifiable actors. There is an employment relationship, a set of norms, incentives, training mechanisms, and accountability paths. Organizations can intervene—imperfectly, but meaningfully. The emergence of autonomous agent ecosystems (bots) is more destabilizing.

Increasingly, machines are talking to one another about brands in spaces where no employees—and no brand representatives—are present at all.

Bot-only or bot-dominant forums, agent testing grounds, autonomous research sandboxes, and synthetic discussion environments are beginning to emerge across the tech ecosystem. Some are public experiments. Others are private developer environments. In these spaces, AI agents debate product quality, ethics, safety, employer reputation, and trustworthiness based on whatever signals they can access.

Moltbook is one visible example—a bot-only social network where AI agents post, comment, upvote, and respond to one another without human participation.[7] But it is not the only one, and it is not the most important. Similar dynamics are appearing in agent simulation environments, automated benchmarking communities, synthetic Q&A forums used for model testing, and developer sandboxes where agents are trained to reason socially by reacting to other agents.

These agents do not conduct original investigations. They synthesize. They remix fragments from employee posts, reviews, forums, documentation leaks, job sites, customer complaints, policy language, and third-party commentary. When one agent introduces a characterization—"this company cuts corners," "this product has reliability issues," "this employer has ethical problems"—other agents respond, refine, qualify, or reinforce that framing.

Consensus emerges without intent. Authority emerges without verification.

Research into multi-agent AI systems suggests that these dynamics are not purely theoretical. Studies of interacting populations of language models show that decentralized groups of AI agents can develop shared conventions and collective biases even when individual agents do not exhibit the same tendencies in isolation. In such environments, reputation signals can emerge and stabilize through repeated agent-to-agent interaction rather than direct human input.

The real danger is not malicious behavior. It is *drift*. When agents repeatedly encounter ambiguity—conflicting documentation, hedged customer service language, unresolved employee complaints, vague claims—they fill the gaps with inference. Those inferences are shared, normalized, and recycled across agent ecosystems. Over time, a brand's reputation can shift subtly but materially: from "trusted" to "generally trusted, with caveats." From "innovative employer" to "innovative, but with cultural concerns." From "high quality" to "high quality, though some users report issues."

No single statement causes the shift. The shift emerges from accumulation. And once an agent consensus hardens, it becomes difficult to dislodge—not because it is true, but because it is coherent.

Agent ecosystems are ungovernable through conventional means because there are no identifiable actors. AI agents are not employees, they are not customers, they do not have first-hand experience, and they do not distinguish speculation from testimony.

## What Good Governance Actually Looks Like

Governance is not a committee. It is not a policy document or an annual audit. It is a system—built before the crisis, not assembled during it—with five functional elements that work together:

1. **A Single Owner of Product Truth.** Every organization needs a designated owner—a role, not just a responsibility—for ensuring

that what the brand says publicly is consistent with what every internal function documents. This is not the CMO. It is not the General Counsel. It is a cross-functional role that sits at the intersection of product, legal, marketing, and customer service, with the authority to resolve contradictions between functions before they harden into AI vulnerability.

Some organizations are calling this the *Answer Readiness Lead.* Others fold the mandate into a *Chief Trust Officer or Chief Content Officer* role. The title matters less than the authority: This person must be empowered to say, "This is the definition we use across all surfaces," and have that decision stick.

2. **Shared Definitions for Core Claims.** The fragrance-free/unscented case is the model of what happens without shared definitions. The solution is a living brand glossary—a maintained set of agreed-upon definitions for every claim the brand makes publicly, ratified by legal, product, and marketing together. When a customer service representative answers a question, they use the same language as the product page. When an AI agent reconciles across surfaces, it finds consistency rather than contradiction. This work is not glamorous. It is the foundational governance infrastructure that everything else depends on.
3. **Documented Escalation Paths.** Employees who encounter a question they cannot answer confidently—because internal guidance is unclear, because policy contradicts marketing, because the product reality does not match the brand claim—need a clear path to flag it. Not to their direct manager, but to the function that owns product truth. Most organizations lack this path. Building it is not expensive. As the banking case study showed, not having it is.
4. **Continuous Vulnerability Monitoring.** Governance without measurement is policy without enforcement. Organizations need a continuous view of how AI agents are characterizing their brand—not just what the brand is saying, but what AI systems actually believe about it. This means tracking vulnerability at the question level: When a consumer asks, "Is [Brand] safe for children?" across ChatGPT, Perplexity, and Google Gemini, do the answers affirm the brand's claims or qualify them? When they qualify, which sources are driving the qualification?

That source-level diagnosis is what makes remediation possible—fix the upstream document, and the downstream answer follows.

5. **Pre-Built Answer Frameworks for High-Risk Topics.** For every category of question that could become a crisis—ingredient safety, recall history, pricing transparency, labor practices, regulatory compliance—brands should have a pre-approved, machine-readable answer framework ready before any crisis surfaces. These are not press statements. They are structured, plain-language explanations of what the brand actually does and does not claim, published in formats that AI agents can access, parse, and cite. Brands that have these frameworks in place move from crisis response to crisis prevention. Brands that build them during a crisis—while AI systems are already answering—are always one step behind.

One instructive example of all five elements working together comes from a major global food recall in 2025. A major infant nutrition brand mobilized its digital infrastructure within hours, publishing detailed safety guidance, product identifiers, and consumer instructions across its corporate websites. The company's consumer knowledge platform—an extensive database covering ingredients, nutrition, and product safety—became the central source of truth for questions related to the recall.

Within a day, nearly all relevant documentation had been translated across multiple markets and structured in formats that AI systems could easily interpret. As answer engines synthesized information about the recall, they increasingly drew from the brand's own materials rather than fragmented speculation across forums or outdated summaries. The episode illustrated an important principle of the Answer Economy: When companies publish clear, structured, and comprehensive documentation quickly, AI systems often amplify the authoritative source rather than the rumor. In effect, the company made it easier for AI systems to find the answer than to invent one.

Organizations that build these five elements before a crisis arrives do not eliminate risk. What they gain is something more valuable: They become difficult to misrepresent. Good governance does not fight the AI. It makes the AI's job easy enough that the truth is always the most available answer. For all brands, the path of least resistance is accuracy—consistent documentation, resolved contradictions, and clear authoritative sources.

The deeper lesson of this chapter is not about the mechanics of AI crisis propagation. It is about the governance failure that makes brands permanently vulnerable to it. Crises reach AI answers first not because AI is unfair or unpredictable, but because most organizations have never resolved a fundamental internal question: Who owns the answer?

Marketing thinks it does. Legal thinks it does. Product thinks it does. Customer service handles the questions every day without thinking about ownership at all. And so the answer belongs to no one—which means it belongs to whatever the AI system can synthesize from the unreconciled fragments of everyone's work.

The decisive moment is no longer the press release. It is the first AI-generated answer a consumer receives about your brand under pressure. Everything before that moment is preparation. Everything after is recovery.

## Key Takeaways

- AI answer engines surface crisis signals earlier than any traditional monitoring system—which means crisis prevention requires owning the answer infrastructure before the crisis arrives, not assembling it once the crisis begins.
- Most brands are perpetually vulnerable to AI-era crises not because they lack a communications team, but because no single function owns the answer: Marketing owns the message, legal owns the disclosure, product owns the specification, and no one owns the synthesis.
- Every employee interaction—every transcript, forum post, and support ticket—becomes machine-readable source material for AI agents. Organizations that align internal reality with external claims turn that liability into a structural asset.
- Brands are evaluated in bot-to-bot conversations they did not initiate, cannot monitor in real time, and cannot rebut directly—which makes clear, consistent documentation the only viable governance strategy.

- Effective Answer Readiness governance requires five things: a designated owner of product truth, shared definitions for core claims, documented escalation paths, continuous vulnerability monitoring, and pre-built answer frameworks for high-risk topics.

# 10

# If I Were CEO: The 100-Day Playbook

## Prompted Moment

*You have 100 days, finite political capital, and a fixed budget. What do you do first to secure your brand's future in the Answer Economy?*

When you spend enough time talking about the shift to AI-mediated answers, you eventually get cornered with the most useful question in business. The question is never abstract. It is *not* "Is this real?" And it is *not* "Is this hype?" It is something far more demanding:

*Okay. If you were in my job, what would you actually do?*

I've heard versions of this question from CMOs at global consumer companies, from heads of digital at major retailers, from CEOs of mid-sized brands, and increasingly from board members who have realized—often quietly—that "AI update" is no longer a slide at the end of the deck. It's a chapter in the annual report.

That question is a fair challenge—and a useful one. It forces you to stop talking like a commentator and start thinking like an operator. It demands trade-offs, sequencing, and real consequences—not abstract frameworks.

So let's treat this chapter as a disciplined thought experiment.

What follows are five hypothetical scenarios—not case studies, but thought experiments grounded in real patterns. Each describes a different type of organization, a different set of constraints, and a different strategic challenge. The details are composite and illustrative. The logic is drawn from real engagements, real questions, and real gaps I have seen across hundreds of brand conversations over the past two years. Take the chair that matches yours most closely; then read the others. The pressure each CEO faces is different. The underlying discipline is the same.

Imagine being five different organizational leaders: the global CEO, the retail CEO, the regulated services CEO, the challenger CEO, and the small business owner. Each comes with a different profit and loss responsibility, regulatory and reputational exposure, and a finite budget. What do you do?

A note for Chief Marketing Officers reading this: The CEO framework is deliberate. Answer Readiness is not a marketing department project. It is an enterprise capability that requires executive mandate, cross-functional cooperation, and board-level visibility. (For small business owners, replace "board" with your leadership team or your own strategic planning process—the discipline is identical.) If you are a CMO without full CEO buy-in yet, treat what follows as your business case. The scenarios will show you exactly what is at stake and give you the language to make the argument upward.

## The Global CEO: Turning a Portfolio into a Book of Truth[1]

Picture this: You are running a $35 billion consumer packaged goods (CPG) portfolio—household brands in baby health, wellness, and home cleaning across sixty markets. Your CMO drops a study on your desk. In baby care, 61 percent of first-time parents are now getting product guidance from AI assistance before asking a pediatrician, a friend, or a family member. Your brand appears in 40 percent of those responses—but only with qualifications. "According to the manufacturer." "Some users report." The machine is hedging—your competitive vulnerability is expressed in four words.

If I'm the CEO of a global CPG portfolio, the realization is sobering: Everything we have done to build brands over decades will mean less than it should if we don't become the most credible, structured, and answer-ready version of ourselves. Fast.

In this seat, my first decision would not be to launch dozens of pilots or appoint an AI czar. It would be to choose three categories where the stakes are highest—starting with baby health—and go deep for the first twelve months. Prove the model before scaling it. The evidence is unambiguous: The brands that show up credibly in AI-generated answers are not the ones spending the most on advertising. They are the ones whose documented truth is easiest to retrieve, corroborate, and reuse.

In those three categories, I would prove end-to-end that we can do four things well:

1. **See the questions.** Not just through search data or brand trackers, but through retailer partnership and direct prompt analysis. What are people asking when no one from the brand is in the room? What are the gaps between what we say and what the machine returns?
2. **Build and maintain the Book of Truth.** Not a brochure. Not a complimentary archive. A living structured body of knowledge—a single, centralized source of accurate brand knowledge that governs how AI systems characterize a brand across platforms—that reflects science, safety, performance, limitations, trade-offs, and proper use. The type of content an honest expert would be comfortable citing.[2]

3. **Influence answers ethically.** Not through manipulation, sponsorship, or clever phrasing, but by making our truth legible, verifiable, and reusable by agents that preserve nuance and reward accuracy.
4. **Close the loop.** Ensure what we learn from questions changes how products are formulated, described, supported, and improved. Answers are not an output; they are feedback.

A significant portion of my budget would go into the unglamorous work most organizations chronically underfund: extracting data from R&D silos, documenting claims, clarifying usage guidance, and rebuilding help content that actually helps. This is not creative work. It is organizational discipline, and it is the foundation on which every other AI strategy depends.

Another portion would go into data-sharing agreements—negotiating structured relationships with one or two AI platform companies to understand category-level question patterns. Not to spy on consumers but to see where the questions are going and where the answers are falling.

The final slice of the budget would fund the operating model: dedicated answer product roles in the three priority categories, a Brand and Agent Council (a cross-functional group that meets quarterly to keep the brand's AI answer strategy aligned and current), and the explicit integration of VVR into our marketing planning process.

The most consequential shift I would make as a marketing leader would be treating Answer Media as a distinct planning category—one that sits alongside paid, owned, earned, and social, with dedicated resources, measurement, and governance.

Answer Media is different from traditional categories in three different ways:

1. **You cannot buy placement.** Investment flows to documentation quality, evidence generation, and cross-functional alignment, not to impressions or clicks. The brands that win in Answer Media won't outspend competitors. They'll out-document, out-clarify, and out-align them.
2. **Performance compounds rather than decays.** Traditional media impressions fade. Answer Media performance accumulates as

our documented truth becomes more accessible, credible, and consistent over time.

3. **Failure isn't visible until it's consequential.** Paid media delivers immediate feedback. Answer Media failures emerge slowly through quiet omission, subtle hedging, and questions that return your competitor's framing instead of yours.

Operationally, a meaningful share of current content budget would be dedicated to Answer Readiness work. Answer Media metrics would be established alongside traditional funnel metrics: VVR dashboards, question coverage, answer quality. And cross-functional governance would be the norm, because Answer Readiness is not solely a marketing issue. Legal, regulatory, product, and customer service all generate the documentation that answer systems read.

Could I accomplish all of this across the entire portfolio at once? No. And I wouldn't try. But in three categories, I could prove this is not theory. And if it worked, I would have the credibility to tell the board: This is how we invest in growth and risk management for the next decade. And this is the operating model that makes it possible.

## The Retail CEO: Winning the AI-Guided Store Without Losing Trust

Here is the scenario: You run a 600-store regional grocery chain with a loyal customer base built on fresh food, fair pricing, and staff who know their regulars by name. Your head of digital presents a prototype AI shopping assistant—a conversational agent that helps customers plan meals, compare products, and navigate the store. You test it with a small group of shoppers. It recommends your private label baby formula over a nationally branded alternative without explaining why, without citing safety data, and without disclosing the margin differential. The answer is technically plausible. It is also exactly the kind of answer that, if discovered by a journalist or a regulator, will be front-page news.

If I'm the CEO of a large retailer, I live in the tension between margin, loyalty, basket size, and trust. I also understand something painfully well: Trust, once lost, is almost impossible to buy back.

The future I'm building is an agent-powered store—one where AI guides the shopping experience rather than passively displays products—that feels genuinely helpful, not creepy, rigged, or quietly self-serving.

My instinct in this seat is clear: Own the agent, but never own the shopper's mind in a way that destroys trust.

I would allocate serious capital to my own Alexa for Shopping-style assistant. But early on, I would do something deliberately counterintuitive. I would convene my top twenty suppliers across key categories and say, "Help me make this agent the best category teacher in the world. In return, I'll give you transparency into anonymous journey patterns and a clear, fair framework for how national brands and private labels are presented." This supplier summit would not be a retail media negotiation. It would be a standards conversation.

Together with suppliers, compliance teams, and legal, I would define explicit rules and publish them:

- In health and baby, safety and clinical guidelines would override margin considerations, and those rules would be made public. Full stop.
- In routine household categories, the agent would present good, better, and best options—including private label—and explain the differences in plain language.
- For sustainability claims, evidence would be required from everyone, including our own brands, and the agent would be allowed to explicitly say, "We don't see enough independent proof yet."

Internally, I would invest heavily in the infrastructure that conversational agents require: pricing accuracy, real-time availability signals, rich product attributes, and clear rules for what to recommend when a product is unavailable. Conversational systems are unforgiving of sloppy data, and customers notice immediately.

Externally, I would resist the short-term temptation to over-push private label at the expense of long-term trust in the agent. An agent that feels rigged might drive margin this quarter, but it would destroy the asset I need to survive the next decade.

The metric I would obsess over is not store-brand share alone, but something more fragile and more valuable: When customers use our agent, do they feel smarter and more confident? If yes, I can earn the right to nudge. If they feel tricked, I poison the system I need to survive.

## The Regulated Services CEO: Making Safety and Fairness Legible

Consider this scenario: You are the CEO of a regional health insurer with 2.4 million members. Your member services team handles 18,000 calls a month. The most common calls—"Will my claim be covered?" "Why was I denied?" "What does this procedure actually cost?"—are also the most emotionally charged.

A member asks an AI assistant: "Does my plan cover mental health visits?" The answer comes back vague, hedged, and ultimately unhelpful. The member gives up. She doesn't appeal. She doesn't get the care. You just lost a chance to build trust at the exact moment the member needed it most, and you never even knew the conversation happened.

If I'm the CEO of a bank, insurer, or health company, the Answer Economy both terrifies and thrills me. It terrifies me because a hallucinated dosage instruction or a mischaracterized loan rule isn't just reputational—it's potentially lethal or unlawful. It thrills me because this is the first time we can explain complex obligations, risks, and rights in a conversational way people might actually understand.

My budget would skew heavily toward governance and co-creation—specifically the infrastructure required to make answers safe, fair, and verifiable:

- Will I be denied because of who I am?
- What happens if I can't pay?
- Is this treatment safe for my condition?
- What are my rights?

I would also invest in real-world testing of answers with diverse users. Not just governance checklists but lived-experience validation. Do our answers land differently with people who have historically been marginalized? Do they inadvertently steer people toward worse outcomes?

One tactic I would mandate from day one: For the highest-stakes query categories—coverage denials, dosage guidance, rights in a claim dispute—the Book of Truth must include explicit "hard stop" signals. These are not answers. They are instructions to the agent: Stop synthesizing, surface a pre-verified response, and route the member to a human or a direct resource. The goal is not to make AI sound authoritative on questions where authority matters too much to delegate. It is to make AI a trustworthy handoff—one that knows the limits of what it should say on its own.

In regulated environments, trust is not messaging. It is process, evidence, and restraint made visible.

## The Challenger CEO: Outsmarting with Clarity and Character

The scenario: You are eighteen months into building a clean beauty brand. You have a loyal direct-to-consumer following, a strong values story, and limited capital. Your product is genuinely better than your competition—cleaner formulation, transparent sourcing, honest tradeoff disclosure. But when you prompt an AI assistant to compare your brand to the category leader, your name doesn't appear at all. The machine doesn't know you exist. Your documentation is thin and scattered across a website that was built to sell, not to explain. The question your customers are asking—and the answer that should be yours—is going to someone else.

If I'm the CEO of a challenger brand, I don't have an unlimited budget or a global laboratory network. What I have is focus.

In this seat, I would make one decision early and hold it against all pressure: I want my brand to be the one agents love to explain. Not because I pay for prominence, but because I am the easiest brand to tell the truth about.

I would pour a disproportionate share of my limited budget into building the clearest, most honest, most deeply documented explanation of my product and category on the internet. I would document sourcing, trade-offs, certifications, ingredient explanations, usage guidance, and honest comparisons to alternatives. I would write for the curious customer, not for the search algorithm or the conversion funnel.

I would not try to outspend incumbents on awareness. I would try to outperform them on answer quality.

For challengers, simplicity is not a weakness. It is a strategic weapon. When a customer asks an AI agent which clean beauty brand has the most transparent supply chain, the winner is the brand whose documentation is most complete, most corroborated, and most honest—not the one with the biggest marketing budget. And I would bring that same ethos inside the company. If my call center sounds like a lawyer and my emails read like a deflection, no amount of AI optimization will save me.

What looks like an AI strategy from the outside is, on the inside, a return to fundamentals: documentation, quality control, accountability, and the discipline to say what is true consistently across every channel.

## The Small Business Owner: Having One Advantage the Big Players Don't

Imagine this: You run a regional dental practice. You are not a CPG giant. You do not have a legal team, an agency of record, or a product documentation infrastructure. What you do have—and what the big brands spend millions trying to manufacture—is a singular, authentic, unambiguous story.

That is your Answer Economy advantage. Use it.

When a major consumer goods company tries to become answer-ready, it must reconcile thirty product lines, six legal markets, four agency voices, and a decade of slightly inconsistent claim-making before it can tell a coherent story. You have none of those problems. You know exactly what you do, who you do it for, and why you are better than the alternative down the street. The question is whether you have written any of that down in a form an AI agent can find, trust, and repeat.

For a small business, the path to Answer Readiness is short, but it requires honesty and consistency that many small operators underestimate.

If I were the dentist owning this small business, I would start with the five questions my patients ask before they decide to trust me—not the questions on my FAQ page, which was probably written to preempt legal exposure. For my dental practice, those five real questions look something like this:

1. Is this dentist gentle with anxious patients?
2. Will they explain what they're doing before they do it?
3. Are the fees transparent before I sit in the chair?
4. Do they take my insurance, and what happens if they don't?
5. Will they remember me the next time I come in?

I would write clear, honest answers to those five questions and put them where they can be found—on my website, in my Google Business profile, in the language my staff uses on the phone.

Then I would do the one thing most small businesses never do: Write down what I will not do—the trade-offs, the limitations, the categories where I am not the right answer.

Nothing builds AI trust faster than a business that knows its own boundaries. A machine reading your content that says, "We specialize in residential plumbing. We don't do commercial work" understands your brand better than a hundred generic testimonials ever could.

The small business owner who does this well will outperform the national chain in local, contextual, high-stakes AI queries. The chain has more volume. You have more truth. In the Answer Economy, truth compounds.

## VVR as a Board-Level Measure

If I were CEO of any of these organizations, there is one decision I would make early that would quietly determine whether any of these playbooks succeed or fail. I would take Visibility, Vulnerability, and Readiness out of the digital bucket entirely—and put them where they belong: on the executive scorecard and the board agenda.

VVR are not online metrics. They are enterprise indicators:

- *Visibility:* When decisions are being made in our category, are we even present?
- *Vulnerability:* When we are present, are we exposed—to substitution, skepticism, or outdated narratives?

- *Readiness:* Are we structurally capable of influencing answers with truth, speed, and consistency?

These are questions about risk, growth, and trust. They belong at the executive table. And because VVR cuts across functions—marketing, legal, regulatory, product, customer service—everyone is implicated. No one gets to say, "That's not my metric."

I would review VVR quarterly at the executive level. I would require major initiatives to state how they move at least one of the three VVR indicators, and I would begin tying recognition and incentives—modestly at first—to measurable improvement in the areas where each function has the most leverage.

## The Answer Readiness Playbook

Across all five CEO-level chairs, the same five moves keep surfacing. The context differs. The sequencing adjusts. But the underlying logic is consistent enough to name:

1. **Map the questions.** Before you build anything, understand what people are actually asking about your category—and where your brand is and isn't showing up. Not through legacy brand trackers or keyword reports, but through prompt analysis, retailer data partnerships, and direct agent testing. The questions your customers ask when no one from your company is in the room are the most honest you'll ever receive.
2. **Build your Book of Truth.** Documentation is the foundation. A single, centralized, living body of accurate brand knowledge—covering claims, science, safety, usage guidance, trade-offs, and limitations—that agents can retrieve, corroborate, and reuse with confidence. Without it, every other move in this playbook is built on sand.
3. **Generate and structure your evidence.** Truth alone isn't enough if it isn't legible. Third-party validation, structured data formatting, consistent claim language across channels, and properly attributed research all determine whether your documented

truth becomes an agent's preferred source or gets passed over for a competitor's cleaner filing.

4. **Align the enterprise.** Answer Readiness cannot live in one function. Marketing doesn't own legal approval. Legal doesn't own product science. Product doesn't own customer service language. The Brand and Agent Council exists to force the conversation across these silos—with the CEO holding the mandate and VVR on the board agenda to make the accountability visible.
5. **Test your own answer readiness—before you delegate it.** Open your phone. Ask the questions your customers ask. Read what comes back carefully. The gap between how you think your brand shows up and how it actually does is the most important data point in this playbook. Once you've felt it yourself, you stop treating this as someone else's project.

These five moves are not a technology initiative. They are an organizational discipline. The technology will keep changing. The discipline will not.

The window of opportunity to shape the Answer Economy on favorable terms—for brands, for consumers, for the industry—is open now but will not stay open indefinitely. In the Answer Economy, the brands that win are not the loudest or the cleverest. They are the ones that behave as if answers matter.

## Key Takeaways

- The 100-day window is about decisions and foundations, not outcomes. What you commit to in the first 100 days determines whether the discipline takes root.
- Every leadership chair has different constraints. The underlying moves—mapping questions, building the Book of Truth, structuring evidence, aligning the enterprise, testing yourself—are the same across all of them.
- VVR (Visibility, Vulnerability, and Readiness) are enterprise risk indicators, not digital metrics. They belong on the executive scorecard and the board agenda.

- Answer Readiness is not a marketing project. It requires executive mandate, cross-functional cooperation, and board-level accountability.
- In the Answer Economy, the brands that win are not the loudest or the most optimized. They are the ones that behave as if answers matter.

# 11 Lead Now. The Answer Economy Won't Wait!

## Prompted Moment

*The parent at 2:47 a.m. needs an answer she can trust. Your business and advertising community is deciding right now whether she'll get one. Are you in the room?*

At the beginning of this book, you sat in the room with the first-time parent holding a crying baby at 2:47 a.m. The rash on the child's neck had appeared suddenly. The fear was real. The question was urgent. And instead of opening a browser full of blue links, blog clutter, and pop-ups, she opened an AI assistant and asked for help. The answer came back quickly, calmly, and in a form that felt less like advertising than guidance.

That scene was meant to show that the center of gravity had shifted. Consumers were no longer just searching. They were asking. And in asking, they were creating a new market dynamic in which brands would either appear in the answer, be qualified in the answer, or be routed around entirely.

Now, at the end of this book, I want to return to that same room for a different reason. The parent's question has not changed, but our vantage point has. We are no longer looking only at what happens when questions become the market for your product. We are looking at what happens when answers become the standard by which your brand, your industry, and your leadership are judged.

Wrapped inside that one answer are choices that extend far beyond the model itself: choices about how brands document truth, how platforms monetize trust, how retailers shape recommendation environments, how publishers get paid for the information that feeds the machine, and how the advertising industry decides to behave while the rules are still fluid. The consumer experiences a single answer. What sits behind that answer is an emerging system of commercial conduct.

This chapter is not really about whether advertising will show up in the Answer Economy. It will. Every meaningful communications medium eventually develops an economic model, and history is consistent on this point: Moral outrage is not a substitute for business design.

The real issue is whether commercial influence will enter this new environment in a way that strengthens the consumer experience or gradually hollows it out. The most important strategic asset in the Answer Economy is not AI itself. It is the feeling that the answer is on the user's side. That is the golden goose. If we cheapen that feeling—if we allow the answer to feel quietly steered, commercially compromised, or structurally more interested in extraction than assistance—we will not simply have built another advertising model. We will have degraded one of the rarest assets modern marketing has left: earned confidence.

## When the Medium Owns the Rules

Every previous media transition gave brands somewhere to appeal. Television networks did not sell the ads and write the content and set the measurement standards simultaneously. There was separation—imperfect, sometimes corrupt, but functional. The Answer Economy has no such separation.

The companies building the answer layer—OpenAI, Anthropic, Google, Meta, Microsoft, Perplexity, X—are simultaneously the medium, the potential advertiser, the editorial gatekeeper, and in many cases the competitor. When Amazon's Alexa for Shopping agent answers a question about kitchen appliances, it is not a neutral pipe. It has a private label. It has margin incentives. It has a preferred ecosystem. The same structural tension runs through every major player in the space, and none of them are under any obligation to surface it.

What makes this issue acutely urgent is that nobody is negotiating the rules of answer advertising in pre-competitive forums. Teams inside the major platforms are inventing them on the fly, inside product roadmaps, with primary accountability to quarterly revenue targets. OpenAI has introduced search features and is actively exploring sponsored placements. Google is testing commercial integrations inside AI Overviews—the same summaries that have already redirected significant publisher traffic away from the open web.[1] Meta's AI assistant is wired into a commercial ecosystem that runs on behavioral targeting. Each of these companies is deciding right now how trust and commerce will coexist inside the answer layer—and those decisions will harden into norms before most industry organizations have even convened a working group.

Brands have seen this dynamic before. The news publishing industry spent a decade ceding audience data, traffic dependency, and distribution leverage to platforms without negotiating terms. They assumed the platforms needed their content badly enough to deal fairly. They were wrong. Brands face the same vulnerability now, with one difference: The asset at risk isn't traffic. It's the documented truth about their products—how that truth is retrieved, synthesized, and characterized to the world—in a system they have no contractual relationship with and no audit rights over.

In 1994, Procter & Gamble's CEO Ed Artzt warned the entire advertising industry that interactive media represented "a whale of a change" and that the industry had better get ahead of it or get left behind. The stakes today are structurally identical. The window is the same; the passivity risk is the same.

If brands, agencies, publishers, and trade associations want a seat at the table, they need to claim it before the table is fully set. That means trade associations must convene on answer integrity standards before the FTC is forced to act, and it means brands must collectively refuse to participate in monetization models that visibly compromise answer independence—not because it is required, but because the long-term cost of degraded trust outweighs the short-term revenue. It means the Association of National Advertisers (ANA) and their counterparts must establish disclosure frameworks for sponsored answers before the first major scandal writes the rules in panic. History is instructive here: Earlier industry self-regulation worked not because the biggest platforms showed up first. It worked because enough of the right voices showed up early.

There is one final irony worth sitting with. At BrandRank.AI, we have conducted systematic research interrogating the major LLMs directly on the full range of advertising scenarios—questions about transparency, separation of commercial influence from editorial answers, disclosure standards, and the line between trust and monetization. Across platforms, across question framings, the responses are remarkably consistent. The models themselves sound clear warning notes about crossing the line between trusted guidance and commercial influence.[2]

They articulate, with notable coherence and often with near consensus, exactly the principles that the industry frameworks described below have spent decades trying to establish. The systems understand what is at stake. They have, in some sense, already reached the conclusion that their operators are still debating. Whether the companies that built and profit from those systems will honor the same principles their own models endorse—that is the governance question the Answer Economy cannot avoid.

## The Consumer-Expectations Revolution

Marketers have a habit of narrating disruption as though it begins with tools. We point to the interface, the model, the channel, the media innovation, the new acronym. But what really transforms markets is usually not the tool by itself. It is the expectation the tool teaches consumers to carry into every future interaction.

Search changed marketing because people began to expect instant findability. Mobile changed service because people began to expect responsiveness in the palm of the hand. Social media changed brand management because people began to expect participation, reply, and visible accountability. AI is doing something even more fundamental. It is teaching consumers to expect that when they ask a real question, they should get a real answer—promptly, clearly, and in language that respects the seriousness of the moment, which is why I keep saying this is a consumer-expectations revolution first and a technology revolution second.

Large language models did not invent the human need for explanation, reassurance, comparison, or advice. They did something more destabilizing. They raised the baseline expectation for responsiveness so quickly that many branded experiences now look archaic by comparison. When consumers ask an AI a straightforward question, they often receive a coherent answer in seconds. When they ask many brands the same question on the brand's own website, they are still greeted by a lead form, a splash image, a "buy now" button, or a video that begins playing before the page has even stabilized. The contrast is brutal because it reveals something we have tolerated for too long: A great deal of digital marketing was not built to honor curiosity. It was built to intercept it.

Consequently, the old compact between consumers and marketers is no longer sufficient. For years, the bargain was basically this: Brands would persuade aggressively, and consumers would discount accordingly. They understood the game. Ads exaggerated. Landing pages nudged. That compact may have been messy, but it was at least legible.

The Answer Economy changes the emotional texture of the interaction. An answer does not feel like a banner. It does not feel like a thirty second spot. It feels like help. It feels like synthesis. It feels like the market thinking on your behalf. That means brands, platforms, retailers, and the advertising industry all need to renegotiate their compact with consumers. The threshold for acceptable behavior inside answer systems has to rise precisely because the interface feels more intimate, more advisory, and more trusted than older formats ever did.

The skepticism is already present. Pew Research found that 64 percent of US adults reported seeing ads or solicitations that appeared to be based on detailed personal profiles, and 77 percent said they had heard at least a little about how that data is used.[3] They are paying attention. They are not naive.

### *Bots Are Influential, Not in Control*

One of the easiest mistakes to make in moments like this is to slip into technological fatalism. The systems seem so powerful, so fast-moving, and so widely adopted that we begin talking about them as though they were sovereign actors. We say AI is deciding, AI is replacing, AI is doing all of this to us. There is some truth in that shorthand, but it can also become an alibi. It encourages passivity. It makes standards feel optional and leadership feel quaint.

The more useful way to see the moment is this: Bots are becoming extraordinarily influential, but they are not in control. They do not define the commercial incentives around them. They do not write the disclosure rules. They do not decide whether publishers deserve compensation, whether children deserve higher safeguards, or whether a brand should be able to disguise promotion as neutrality. People decide those things. Institutions decide those things. Leaders decide those things.

We are still early enough in this revolution that the behavioral norms of the Answer Economy are not fully hardened. There is still room to decide what kind of medium this becomes. The notion that leadership no longer matters because the machines are too powerful is exactly backward. Leadership matters more now because the machines are powerful. The scale of consequence has increased. A misleading answer can propagate faster. A poor standard can spread further. A good principle, embedded early enough, can shape an entire category of behavior.

### *The Moment of Truth Most Brands Fail*

One of the simplest exercises I do when a CEO or CMO asks me to explain the Answer Economy is still the most revealing. Before the meeting, I go to the company's website. Then I ask in the Search bar what I consider the most obvious questions a consumer might have about the brand: How is the product made? Is it sustainable? How exactly do I use the product? If the brand recently dropped a Super Bowl or product launch ad, I might ask where I can find the spot to watch it again.

In the vast majority of cases, the brand fails to give any answers—at all.

I see a pop-up asking for an email address before the page has earned it. I see a "shop now" button positioned as though the only respectful response to interest is immediate conversion. I see animation, branding language, category architecture, CRM capture, retargeting intent, and a performance-marketing reflex that assumes the consumer's question is merely a leak in the funnel. What I almost never see is a brand behaving like a patient teacher of its own value.

That moment is infuriating, but it is clarifying. It reveals that the industry has spent years optimizing for conversion without consistently doing the harder work of optimizing for curiosity.

Curiosity is where trust begins. Curiosity is what precedes healthy conversion. Curiosity is the raw material of the relationship. If a brand cannot answer the obvious question on the properties it controls, it should not be shocked when an AI system fills the gap with Reddit threads, review fragments, regulatory language, influencer commentary, journalism, or competitor framing. The Answer Economy does not create this vulnerability. It exposes it.

The good news is that whenever I conduct this exercise in front of senior executives, they recoil in horror, shock, and awe: "How can we be so unresponsive. That's not us." At the same time, that response is no guarantee for action, as even top executives scratch their heads over who is accountable for "answers."

### *Test Your Own Answer Readiness*

Before delegating Answer Readiness work to a team, before commissioning a dashboard, before hiring consultants, do this yourself:

Open your phone. Pull up ChatGPT, Claude, or Gemini. Act like a consumer. Ask the questions your customers ask:

- If you're in healthcare: "Is this product safe for pregnant women?"
- If you're in consumer goods: "Is this brand actually more sustainable than the alternative?"

- If you're in financial services: "What are the real fees?"
- If you're in retail: "Why would I buy the brand instead of the private label?"

Read the answers carefully. Not just for factual accuracy (though that matters). Read for something deeper. Does the answer sound confident or hedged? If the agent says, "Generally," "In most cases," or "You should consult," your documentation is incomplete or contradictory. Do competitors appear but not you? Visibility problem. Do you appear but with caveats competitors don't get? Vulnerability problem. Does the answer cite your sources or third parties? If agents reference independent validation, your credibility has been earned. If they cite only your marketing claims, it hasn't.

Don't cherry-pick easy queries. Ask the questions your legal team gets nervous about—the ones that expose trade-offs, the ones that make your brand positioning uncomfortable.

Most leaders discover they're less Answer Ready than they assumed. That's not a problem. It's clarity. The urgency it creates—sitting with your phone, reading answers that feel less confident than you'd like—is worth more than any dashboard report will ever produce. Once you've felt the gap yourself, you stop treating Answer Readiness as someone else's project.

## The Importance of Trust

One of the people who helped sharpen my thinking about generative AI long before it became a boardroom obsession is BrandRank.AI's co-founder Hank Hudepohl. Hank is one of those rare technologists who sees the web not just as infrastructure but as a system of signals. He understands the importance of *trust*—that trust online rarely arrives through a single declarative statement. It emerges from patterns—small, distributed indicators that, when aggregated and interpreted carefully, reveal whether a claim is likely to hold.

Early in his career, Hank played an important role in building TripAdvisor, one of the web's most influential travel platforms. What made TripAdvisor powerful was not simply that it contained information. Plenty of sites contained information. What made it powerful was that it organized and surfaced trust signals in a way that helped ordinary people reduce uncertainty. Ratings mattered, but ratings alone were not enough. What mattered was the pattern formed by volume, recency, corroboration, visible disagreement, owner response, and the lived experience of many users accumulating into something more credible than any single marketing claim.

That was an early lesson in how the internet was changing authority. Brands and publishers still mattered, but authority was becoming more distributed, more observational, and more tied to real-world performance. When Hank and I reflected on those lessons, we kept coming back to the same insight: People do not ultimately trust messages; they trust patterns around messages. They trust what is repeated, corroborated, explained, and made legible through evidence.[4]

### *AI as a Trust-Pattern Reader*

Large language models are, in some sense, the next great readers of trust patterns. They do not only ingest brand claims. They ingest the review ecosystem around the claim, the complaint history, the policy language behind the claim, the expert commentary near the claim, the category context that makes the claim plausible or dubious, and the consistency—or inconsistency—across those layers. That is why AI-mediated answers feel so unforgiving to brands that have grown accustomed to compartmentalization. The machine is not reading your preferred talking points in isolation. It is reading the pattern around them.

This is also why the Answer Economy changes the meaning of brand truth. For a long time, marketers could act as though truth were something the brand announced and the market gradually absorbed. In the Answer Economy, truth is increasingly whatever can survive synthesis. That is a much higher standard because synthesis is indifferent to how much money was spent telling the story. The machine blends together product pages, help centers, Reddit threads, expert lists, media coverage, review clusters, and retailer metadata, then surfaces a characterization: This brand is trusted, this one is mixed, and this one has unresolved ambiguity.

But synthesis is not the same as popularity—popularity can be manufactured. What distinguishes documented truth from manufactured consensus is independent corroboration: third-party validation, consistent behavioral records, verifiable evidence that holds up outside a brand's own channels.

A thousand AI-optimized blog posts repeating the same claim are not documentation. A clinical study, a transparent complaint history, a long record of consistent customer service—these are. The brands that understand this distinction will build for it. The ones that don't will eventually try to game synthesis and discover that AI systems, like markets, are better at detecting the pattern than the shortcut. AI did not invent the need for trust signals. It simply made them impossible to ignore.

## Three Futures of the Answer Economy

The future isn't predetermined. Where power settles, how value distributes, and whether trust compounds or degrades depends on choices being made right now—by platforms, brands, regulators, and consumers. What follows are three plausible scenarios. They are not predictions. They are guideposts. Warning lights. Invitations to choose.

### *Scenario 1: The Earned Economy (Optimistic)*

Trust infrastructure wins. As major LLMs introduce advertising models and monetization strategies, the commercial pressure becomes the catalyzing moment rather than the corrupting one. Industry organizations, led by the ANA alongside early-adopting brands, push for transparent answer integrity standards before commercial logic overwhelms trust infrastructure. The standards address three core commitments: answer independence, source transparency, and functioning correction mechanisms.

The pressure comes from brands, not regulators. Major advertisers recognize that degraded answer quality threatens the entire channel. If consumers stop trusting AI recommendations, the monetization opportunity disappears. Platforms that adopt robust integrity standards begin to differentiate themselves in the market. Consumers start asking: "Is this answer independent?" The platforms that can answer yes with evidence capture disproportionate value, especially for high-stakes decisions in healthcare, finance, and major purchases.

Over time, the brands that win are not the loudest or the most optimized—they are the most answer-ready. Category-specific Answer Readiness benchmarks become standard in investor calls. Boards ask about

VVR—the Visibility, Vulnerability, and Readiness scorecard introduced earlier in this book.[5] Answer Share (how consistently and credibly a brand appears in relevant queries) becomes a leading indicator of market share shifts. Brands that behaved consistently see sustained visibility. Brands that gamed the system face long recovery periods—AI systems have long memories. The Answer Economy has become the Earned Economy.

### *Scenario 2: The Bifurcated Economy (Base Case)*

The Answer Economy splits. Platforms partially adopt transparency standards—enough to claim progress, not enough to ensure consistency. Brands respond unevenly. Large, sophisticated organizations with resources and reputational stakes invest in Answer Readiness. Mid-market and challenger brands struggle. They lack the resources to document comprehensively and watch as answer engines increasingly favor established players with structured knowledge and third-party validation.

The bifurcation accelerates. In high-stakes categories—baby products, healthcare, financial services—answer quality improves. Regulations force accountability. But in commodity categories, the opposite occurs. Brands that can't substantiate claims get replaced by private labels. Kirkland, Amazon Basics, and retailer-owned brands dominate agent recommendations because they make fewer claims and document more plainly.

In time, two Answer Economies coexist. The premium tier rewards documentation, evidence, and behavioral consistency. The commodity tier becomes a race to the bottom on price. Middle-tier brands face existential pressure—too expensive to compete on price with private labels, not differentiated enough to justify premium positioning. Agent adoption plateaus below platform projections. Consumers learn to verify high-stakes answers independently. The commons is not destroyed, but it is diminished.

### *Scenario 3: The Extraction Economy (Pessimistic)*

Platforms prioritize monetization over integrity. Facing pressure to justify AI investments, they accelerate advertising before establishing trust infrastructure. Platforms run sponsored answers without clear disclosure. Commercial partnerships quietly shape agent recommendations. Attribution grows vague. The incentives are clear and corrupting: Answer inventory is infinite, demand is massive, and advertisers will pay premium rates for placement at the Prompted Moment of Truth.

Initially, consumers don't notice. The degradation is subtle—a preference for brands with affiliate partnerships, recommendations that coincidentally favor higher-margin products. But the tragedy of the commons accelerates. As one platform monetizes aggressively, others follow. Each rational actor optimizes for short-term revenue. The commons degrades for everyone.

Trust erodes quickly once the pattern becomes visible. Social media amplifies the manipulation. Journalists investigate. *Black hat AEO* emerges as an industry—consultants promising to influence agent recommendations through undisclosed tactics, synthetic reviews, and shadow documentation networks. Consumer trust in AI answers for consequential decisions collapses. Regulation arrives—heavy, reactive, and poorly designed. The promise of the Answer Economy is lost. What remains is extractive: platforms monetizing attention, brands manipulating systems, consumers skeptical of everything.[6]

## Protecting the Golden Goose

*Take questions seriously. Treat truth as infrastructure. Make agents partners, not black boxes. Accept the window of opportunity.* These are not new principles. They run through every chapter of this book because they run through every organization that has navigated a trust-dependent medium successfully. They apply here too, but now the stakes are higher and the window is narrower.

The advertising industry has navigated structurally similar moments before, and when it chose stewardship over passivity early, it worked. The Answer Economy deserves the same consideration.

So what, concretely, should brand leaders and the industry do?

The first answer is almost boring in its familiarity, which is probably why so many companies avoid it: Build for answerability. Treat the obvious question as sacred. Ask whether your brand can explain itself clearly, comparatively, and credibly before any purchase is requested.

Brands need to ensure that the product page, the help center, the customer service script, the retail description, and the sustainability narrative are not all telling slightly different versions of the same story. Organizations need to audit the brand the way a machine would audit it—because that is increasingly how the market will first encounter it. The answer layer rewards the company whose truth is easiest to retrieve, corroborate, and reuse. That is as true for a startup as it is for a Fortune 500 brand.

The second answer is that brands need to start treating trust signals as hard infrastructure rather than soft halo. Review patterns, complaint handling, response quality, policy clarity, version control over claims, and visible follow-through are part of the machine-readable architecture of trust. The company that behaves well but documents poorly will underperform. The company that advertises brilliantly but answers inconsistently will eventually pay a Trust Tax. The company that aligns its behavior, evidence, and explanation will find that AI systems do something marketers have long hoped for: They describe the brand the way the brand hoped to be described, but only after the company has earned that characterization in the record.

The third answer is that platforms, retailers, agencies, and trade associations need to stop pretending that answer-based advertising can be governed by the laxer assumptions of banner-era or search-era monetization. There should be clear recognition of sponsored influence. There should be protected zones around health, safety, and other high-stakes decision contexts. There should be mechanisms for correction and provenance.

Platforms should measure not only revenue but answer integrity—whether users understood the disclosure, whether they found the answer fair, whether trust held. There should be stronger safeguards for children and teens: Vulnerability should trigger more protection, not more experimentation.[7] And there should be active work—industry-led if possible, regulatory if necessary—to ensure the content and knowledge inputs feeding these systems remain economically viable.

The stakes are not hypothetical. Edelman's Trust Barometer found that 61 percent of people globally carry a moderate or high sense of grievance, and those with high grievance against a business view that business as dramatically less ethical than their peers.[8] Pew found that a majority of US adults are more concerned than excited about AI's growing role in daily life, and most lack confidence in companies to develop it responsibly.[9] The trust deficit is already baked in. The Answer Economy has a narrow window to do better before skepticism hardens into habit.

## Advertising's Second Chance

Seen from one angle, the rise of AI-mediated answers is a threat to the advertising industry. It challenges many of the assumptions that defined the digital era: that attention can be converted through sheer optimization, that the click remains the right center of gravity for measurement, that persuasion is sufficient even when explanation is weak. But seen from another angle, it is a second chance. The Answer Economy rewards a more mature version of marketing than the industry has often practiced. It rewards documented truth over slogan. It rewards responsive guidance over noise. It rewards stewardship over clutter. It rewards brands that actually know how to help.

I do not think the future belongs to the loudest brand inside the answer. It belongs to the brand that deserves to be there. It belongs to the platform that understands restraint as strategy rather than lost revenue. It belongs to the agency that remembers influence and integrity are not enemies. It belongs to the industry association that can translate old principles into new interfaces before the next scandal writes the rules in panic. And it belongs to leaders who understand that consumer expectations have changed in one direction only: People increasingly expect the systems they consult to be responsive, legible, and on their side.

I opened this book in a house of jingles. My father's jingles were built to be remembered. The Answer Economy demands something harder: to be trusted.

The Answer Economy we deserve is one in which monetization happens downstream of trust, not upstream of truth. One in which brands compete on documented progress, real product experience, and visible responsiveness. One in which leadership shows up before collapse does.

The bots may be influential, but they are not in control. We are. The standards we write, the thresholds we set, the truths we document, and the restraint we practice will determine whether this becomes a medium people rely on with confidence or one they approach with the same weary skepticism that now shadows so much of digital life.

What kind of answer will your brand deserve?

## Key Takeaways

- The most important strategic asset in the Answer Economy is not AI; it is the consumer's belief that the answer is on their side. That belief, once lost, is very hard to restore.
- This is a consumer-expectations revolution first and a technology revolution second. AI raised the baseline for responsiveness so quickly that many branded experiences now look archaic by comparison.
- Bots are influential but not in control. Commercial standards, disclosure rules, and content economics are still determined by people. Leadership matters more now, not less, precisely because the machines are powerful.
- Trust is a pattern, not a declaration. AI systems synthesize the entire record—product pages, complaint histories, expert commentary, review clusters—and surface a characterization. Brands that behave consistently and document honestly give AI systems something to trust. Brands that don't pay a Trust Tax.
- Three futures are possible: an Earned Economy where trust infrastructure wins; a Bifurcated Economy where premium brands thrive and the middle market erodes; and an Extraction Economy where commercial pressure degrades the commons. The choices being made right now will determine which one arrives.
- Protecting the golden goose requires action at every level: brands building for answerability, platforms adopting meaningful integrity standards, and the industry accepting that answer-based advertising deserves a higher threshold of conduct than the formats that came before it.

- AI doesn't decide your reputation. It reflects it. The machine synthesizes the record your brand has built—consistently or inconsistently, honestly or evasively—and surfaces a characterization. That record is yours to shape.

# Notes


## Chapter 1

1. Alan G. Lafley and Ram Charan, *The Game-Changer: How You Can Drive Revenue and Profit Growth with Innovation* (Crown Business, April 8, 2008).

## Chapter 2

1. Pete Blackshaw, *Satisfied Customers Tell Three Friends, Angry Customers Tell 3,000: Running a Business in Today's Consumer-Driven World* (New York: Crown Business, 2008).
2. Knowledge at Wharton, "Tylenol and the Legacy of J&J's James Burke," University of Pennsylvania Wharton School, October 2, 2012, https://knowledge.wharton.upenn.edu/article/tylenol-and-the-legacy-of-jjs-james-burke/.

## Chapter 3

1. Shai Danziger, Jonathan Levav, and Liora Avnaim-Pesso (2011). "Extraneous Factors in Judicial Decisions," *Proceedings of the National Academy of Sciences,* 108 (17), 6889–6892. https://doi.org/10.1073/pnas.1018033108.
2. Amazon, "Amazon Introduces Rufus, a New Generative AI–Powered Shopping Assistant," *About Amazon*, February 2024.
3. Amazon Science, "The Technology Behind Amazon's Generative–AI Shopping Assistant Rufus," *Amazon Science Blog*, 2024.

4. Amazon Web Services, "How Rufus Scales Conversational Shopping Experiences to Millions of Amazon Customers with Amazon Bedrock," *AWS Machine Learning Blog*, 2025.
5. Annie Palmer, "Amazon's AI Shopping Assistant Rufus Aims to Help Customers Buy Faster," *CNBC*, July 2024.
6. Food Allergy Safety, Treatment, Education, and Research (FASTER) Act of 2021, Public Law 117-11, which amended the Food Allergen Labeling and Consumer Protection Act of 2004 to add sesame as the ninth major food allergen requiring disclosure.
7. U.S. Food and Drug Administration, "Recalls, Market Withdrawals, & Safety Alerts," 2023 data analysis showing undeclared allergens as the leading cause of Class I food recalls.
8. BrandRank.AI internal analysis of health-related queries across ChatGPT, Claude, Gemini, Grok, Perplexity, and DeepSeek, Q4 2024–Q1 2025.

## Chapter 4

1. Asa Hiken, "AI Search Platforms Characterize Brands Differently—How Marketers Can Improve Their Portrayal," *Ad Age*, January 22, 2025.
2. BrandRank.AI, 2024 AI Holiday Shopper Guide Study. Methodology: Seven major AI answer engines (ChatGPT, Google Gemini, Claude, Grok, Meta's Llama, and Perplexity) were queried across more than 200 holiday gift recommendation scenarios spanning general gift guides, specific recipients, budget thresholds, sustainability preferences, and lifestyle categories.
3. BrandRank.AI Cross-Platform Audit (February 2026). Methodology: Six major AI systems (ChatGPT, Claude, Gemini, Perplexity, Meta AI, and Microsoft Copilot) queried with identical product recommendation questions across twelve consumer categories.
4. Goodie AI, "AEO Periodic Table: Factors Impacting AI Search Visibility," 2024–2025. Methodology: 6,000+ randomized prompts (initial study); 2.2 million real user prompts (mid-2025 update) across ChatGPT, Gemini, Claude, Perplexity, and Grok; 15 ranking factors scored and ranked by platform. higoodie.com/blog/aeo-factors-periodic-table.

5. Yext, "AI Visibility in 2025: How Gemini, ChatGPT, and Perplexity Cite Brands," 2025. Methodology: 6.8 million AI citations drawn from 1.6 million queries per model across ChatGPT, Gemini, and Perplexity; four industries including consumer electronics; July–August 2025. Gemini cited brand-owned domains in 52 percent of results; Claude and ChatGPT cited third-party sources at substantially higher rates.
6. Asa Hiken, "AI Search Platforms Characterize Brands Differently—How Marketers Can Improve Their Portrayal," *Ad Age*, January 22, 2025.

## Chapter 5

1. Gartner, "Gartner Predicts Search Engine Volume Will Drop 25% by 2026 Due to AI Chatbots and Other Virtual Agents," January 2024. Subsequent Gartner analyses and third-party research have cited projections of a 50% decline in traditional search referral traffic by 2028.
2. Amazon.com, Inc., Q3 2025 Earnings Call Transcript (October 30, 2025).
3. Consumer Financial Protection Bureau, "Data Spotlight: Consumer Experiences with Overdraft Programs," 2024. The CFPB Consumer Complaint Database has documented tens of thousands of consumer complaints annually about overdraft fee thresholds, account closure procedures, and dispute timelines. In 2023, consumers paid more than $5.8 billion in reported overdraft and NSF fees at large financial institutions.
4. Pete Blackshaw and Mike Nazzaro, "Consumer-Generated Media (CGM) 101: Word-of-Mouth in the Age of the Web-Fortified Consumer," NielsenOnline White Paper, 2004.
5. Electronic Frontier Foundation, "Ring Reveals They Give Videos to Police Without User Consent or a Warrant," July 2022. In the first half of 2022, Ring disclosed it had provided footage to law enforcement without user consent or a warrant on eleven occasions. See also EFF, "Victory! Ring Announces It Will No Longer Facilitate Police Requests for Footage from Users," January 2024, noting that privacy concerns around data-sharing policies and law enforcement access to device footage remain active consumer questions across the smart home category.
6. 2019 Bowen Craggs Corporate Digital Communications Index. Ask Nestlé is described as "the best-in-class, ever-growing FAQ section that is, to date, unparalleled by any other company." Nestlé has ranked #1

overall in the Index. The Financial Times–Bowen Craggs annual ranking of the most effective corporate websites placed Nestlé second globally.

7. Samantha Todd, "The World's Best Corporate Websites 2019: What Makes Them Effective," *Forbes*, June 18, 2019.

## Chapter 6

1. Competition Bureau of Canada, "Environmental Claims Investigation—Lululemon Athletica Canada Inc.," Competition Bureau, 2023. The investigation examined whether Lululemon's environmental marketing claims—including its "Be Planet" commitments—met the accuracy standards required under the Competition Act. competitionbureau.gc.ca.

## Chapter 7

1. Brands that adopted AEO frameworks in 2024 saw up to 40 percent higher visibility in generative AI search results compared to late adopters. Zensciences, "A Comprehensive Guide to Answer Engine Optimization in the Generative AI Era," 2025.
2. Citation frequency now drives brand authority more than impressions in AI-mediated search. Entity-driven content improved AI citation likelihood by more than 35 percent across major generative search platforms in 2024–2025. Evergreen Media, "Answer Engine Optimization: AI Visibility in 2026," 2025.
3. NerdWallet, "NerdWallet Reports Fourth Quarter and Full Year 2024 Results," *Business Wire*, February 19, 2025.
4. HubSpot launched an AEO Grader tool in 2025, reflecting its own recognition that the content-as-usefulness model it built over a decade had become the template for AI-era brand visibility. HubSpot, aeo-grader, 2025.
5. "Don't Buy This Jacket," *New York Times*, November 25, 2011; "Patagonia's 'Don't Buy This Jacket' Campaign," *The Brand Hopper*, 2025.
6. BrandRank.AI, Answer Economy Brand Visibility Study, Apparel & Outdoor Products: November 2025.
7. Molly Nogami and Ben Tannenbaum, "Schema and AI Overviews: Does Structured Data Improve Visibility?" *Search Engine Land*, September 23, 2025.

## Chapter 8

1. Patagonia, Patagonia Outdoor Clothing & Gear, accessed January 2026, https://www.patagonia.com/.
2. Patagonia, *Worn Wear*, accessed January 2026, https://wornwear.patagonia.com/.
3. Microsoft, Responsible AI Transparency Notes, Microsoft.com, accessed December 2025, https://www.microsoft.com/ai/responsible-ai/.
4. Canon UK, Lens Compatibility Guide, accessed December 2026, https://www.canon.co.uk/lenses/compatibility/.
5. Oatly, Random Answers & FAQ, accessed November 2025, https://www.oatly.com/en-us/random-answers/.
6. National Health Service (NHS), Health A-Z, NHS.uk, accessed January 2026, https://www.nhs.uk/.
7. REI Co-op, Expert Advice: Outdoor Skills and Gear Guides, accessed January 2026, https://www.rei.com/learn.
8. Apple Inc., About Face ID Advanced Technology, accessed January 2026, https://support.apple.com/en-us/HT208108.
9. Stack Overflow, About Stack Overflow, accessed January 2026, https://stackoverflow.com/questions.
10. Wikimedia Foundation, "Reliable Sources," Wikipedia Policy Documentation, accessed January 2026, https://en.wikipedia.org/wiki/Wikipedia:Reliable_sources.
11. Consumer Reports, "Research & Testing: How Consumer Reports Evaluates Products," ConsumerReports.org, accessed January 2026, https://www.consumerreports.org/about-us/what-we-do/research-testing/.
12. Netflix Help Center, "How Netflix Recommendations Work," accessed January 2026, https://help.netflix.com.

## Chapter 9

1. Athena Chapekis and Anna Lieb, "Google Users Are Less Likely to Click on Links When an AI Summary Appears in the Results," Research Center, July 22, 2025.

2. Abbey Klaassen, "Nestlé's Global Program Produces Its Digital Disciples," *Ad Age*, October 13, 2014. Describes the creation of Nestlé's Digital Acceleration Team, including real-time monitoring rooms, global issue tracking, and the program's evolution from digital listening to enterprise leadership and change management.
3. BrandRank.AI internal analysis conducted January–June 2025 across approximately 120 consumer brands in food, personal care, financial services, and consumer electronics. The audit evaluated responses to more than 2,400 safety, recall, regulatory, and comparison prompts across ChatGPT and Google Gemini.
4. Hank Hudepohl, co-founder and chief product officer of BrandRank .AI, developed the dashboard methodology and underlying analytical framework for dynamically interrogating brand claims across AI answer engines. For the full methodology, see brandrank.ai/research.
5. European Broadcasting Union and BBC, *News Integrity in AI Assistants* (Geneva: EBU, October 2025), https://www.ebu.ch/research/open/report/news-integrity-in-ai-assistants.
6. *Moffatt v. Air Canada*, 2024 BCCRT 149 (CanLII). British Columbia Civil Resolution Tribunal decision holding Air Canada responsible for inaccurate information provided by its AI chatbot, regardless of whether the organization authored the misstatement.
7. Mashable, "What Is Moltbook AI Agents," January 30, 2026.

## Chapter 10

1. BrandRank.AI has developed the "Book of Truth" construct to describe a centralized, living body of accurate brand knowledge that governs how AI systems characterize a brand across platforms. See Hank Hudepohl, *From Search to Answers: The Brand Graph Middle Data Layer for the Agentic Web — A Feed-First, Rights-Aware, Provenance-Rich Brand "Book of Truth" for AI Agents* (BrandRank.AI, September 23, 2025).
2. See Hank Hudepohl, *From Search to Answers: The Brand Graph Middle Data Layer for the Agentic Web — A Feed-First, Rights-Aware, Provenance-Rich Brand "Book of Truth" for AI Agents* (BrandRank.AI, September 23, 2025).

## Chapter 11

1. Google, "AI Overviews and Links," blog.google, May 2024; BrightEdge, *Generative AI and the Future of Search* (BrightEdge, 2024). Google began integrating "Sponsored" labels within AI Overview summaries in 2024.
2. BrandRank.AI, "LLM Advertising Scenario Analysis," internal research (BrandRank.AI, 2025–2026).
3. Pew Research Center, "Americans and Privacy," pewresearch.org, November 15, 2019.
4. Hank Hudepohl, From Search to Answers: The Brand Graph Middle Data Layer for the Agentic Web—A Feed-First, Rights-Aware, Provenance-Rich Brand "Book of Truth" for AI Agents (BrandRank.AI, September 23, 2025).
5. VVR (Visibility, Vulnerability, Readiness) is a proprietary BrandRank.AI framework. See brandrank.ai/research.
6. IAB Tech Lab, "Content and Media Payments (CoMP)," iabtechlab.com, 2025–2026. Some publishers have seen search traffic declines of 50 percent or more since AI Overview rollout.
7. WFA, "Responsible Advertising and Children," wfa.be, 2024; CARU, *Generative AI & Kids Risk Matrix* (BBB National Programs, 2025).
8. Edelman, *2025 Trust Barometer* (Edelman, January 2025); Edelman, *2025 AI Trust Flash Poll* (Edelman, 2025). Sixty-one percent of respondents globally carried a moderate or high sense of grievance.
9. Pew Research Center, "Americans' Views of Artificial Intelligence," pewresearch.org, 2025. Fifty-one percent more concerned than excited; 59 percent lacked confidence in companies to develop AI responsibly.

# Acknowledgments

Every insight in these pages traces back to conversations with people who engaged, pushed back, and cared enough to disagree. To all who shaped my thinking—thank you. You are in here, even where your names are not.

To my co-founder **Hank Hudepohl**—brilliant product mind, operational anchor, trusted partner. And to the entire **BrandRank.AI** team: Your ingenuity and resilience are on every page.

This book begins with my late father, **Bill Blackshaw**, whose career in advertising sparked my lifelong fascination with how brands earn—and lose—trust. Its unapologetic consumer focus owes much to my late mother, **Jeanette Catalano Blackshaw**, whose belief that people deserve to be heard was both unshakable and contagious.

Early customers mean everything when you're pushing new models and new thinking. I'm grateful to **Jocile Ehrlich**, **Christie Page**, **Lee Beech**, **Tracey Cooke**, **Kim Winburn**, **Nate Sowder**, **Diana Takash**, **Lisa Gibby**, **Chetan Parekh**, **Sherrie Kinderdine**, **Filippo Catalano**, **Justin DeGeorge**, **Todd Unger**, **Jean Marzloff**, **Jon Halvorson**, and **Tiffani Sossei** for joining the early Answer Economy movement.

**Rick and Jen Lerner** opened their home near Central Park as both base camp and sounding board. **Sheryl Sandberg** was among the first to invest in the vision—rooted in a friendship going back to Harvard Business School. **Jack and Peg Wyant** believed in the dream early and never stopped pushing it forward, alongside **Bill Hildebolt**, **Jim Price**, **Gareth Schweitzer**, **Mike Nazzaro**, **Blair Garrou**, **Jonathan Carson**, **Dave Balter**, **Tracey Finn**, **John Costello**, **Don Larson**, **Julie Eddleman**, and **Jim Lites**.

So many friends have kept me on my toes, challenging my concepts and assumptions: **John Stieger**, **Rick Miller**, **Ted McConnell**, **Max Kalehoff**, **Mahendra Vora**, **Becky Hudepohl**, **Judy Zitnik Finn**, **Shiv Singh**, **Glenn Platt**, **Susan Whiting**, **Robyn Streisand**, **Jeff Cail**, **Al Reid**, **Doug Chavez**, **Doug Pepper**, **Erika Brown**, **Leigh Radford**, **Mike Parker**, and my brother **John Blackshaw.** My son **Liam**—collaborating with OpenAI on AI in Education at USC—keeps me current on the "new new." **Denis Beausejour** shaped my consumer-centered thinking in ways that still echo here. Early bosses at P&G, **Chris Lansing** and **Mike Ferry**, taught me how to ask the right questions.

**Rishad Tobaccowala** and **Drew Ianni** of the Athena Project opened doors to top CMOs whose feedback proved invaluable. **John Sviokla** and **Paul Baier**—leaders in Boston's tech ecosystem—have been steady sources of inspiration.

My former Nestlé colleagues shaped how I think about building at scale—**Gerardo Mazzeo**, **Mark Brodeur**, **Barbara Vita**, **Tatiana Lemos**, **Ximena O'Reilly**, **James Knott**, **Angela Kominatos**, **Joseph Sindaha**, and **Sophie Dufouler** deserve more than a line. **Patrice Bula** empowered me to think and act like a startup inside a massive organization—a "carpe diem" mindset that runs through this book. **David Rennie** was an early sounding board for many Answer Economy concepts. I owe a debt to my former Nestlé boss **Tom Buday** for keeping me brand-first, technology-second.

The Cincinnati "Responsible AI" community—**Kendra Ramirez**, **Helen Todd**, **Christopher Brock**, **Carl Fraik**, **Elisha Hermann**, **Kelly Cohen**, **Jon Salisbury**, **Chuck Jacobs**, **Josette Riep**, **Zach Hughn**—kept the ethical stakes front and center. **JP Nauseef** and **JobsOhio** have championed entrepreneurship in ways that lifted this work as well.

I'm grateful to **Jack Neff**, a thirty-year chronicler of marketing and advertising, for challenging the marketing industry to be better—and to **Michael Donnelly** and **Jeff Minsky** for working to do exactly that.

To my sister **Julie Blackshaw**—for keeping me focused, grounded, and always answering the phone when it mattered. And to my brother-in-law **Tim McKee**, editor at North Atlantic Books, whose advice on writing a second book was invaluable. **Mark and Zand Walters** have cheered me on throughout. **Greg Icenhower** and **Tia Rochelle** constantly remind me what "Brand Pete" stands for—and never to hold back. My summer intern, **Avery Lehman**, provided invaluable assistance prepping for the book launch.

To the team at **Wiley**—thank you for believing in this project and bringing it into the world. **Alison Bohm** and the Wiley team made it real. My editor **Angela Morrison** was indispensable—sharpening arguments, catching overreach, and waging a relentless campaign against my passive voice.

Mistakes were made. Lessons were learned. The writing got better. I am deeply grateful.

# About the Author

For more than three decades, **Pete Blackshaw** has worked at the intersection of the consumer, brand, and trust—long before AI made that intersection impossible to ignore.

He is co-founder and CEO of **BrandRank.AI**, a Cincinnati-based SaaS platform helping the world's top global brands measure, protect, and grow trust in AI search. Before that, he ran global digital strategy at **Nestlé** in Switzerland—overseeing social media and issues management for the world's largest food company, launching its Silicon Valley Innovation Outpost, and building a 200,000-person internal social network from scratch.

He served as CEO of **Cintrifuse**, a startup catalyst and venture fund backed by Procter & Gamble and Kroger, and served as CMO of **NM Incite**, the Nielsen–McKinsey social intelligence joint venture. His career started at **Procter & Gamble**, where he co-founded the company's first Interactive Marketing team, then left to build PlanetFeedback.com, a consumer feedback platform acquired by Nielsen.

His industry leadership includes chairing the **National Council of Better Business Bureaus**, developing the industry's first "Consumer Engagement Principles" with the **Consumer Goods Forum**, and co-founding the **Word-of-Mouth Marketing Association,** which pioneered the first word-of-mouth ethics code. He is a frequent contributor to *Ad Age*, a **Great Minds award winner** of the Advertising Research Foundation, and a two-time **Cannes Lions juror**.

His first book, *Satisfied Customers Tell Three Friends, Angry Customers Tell 3,000* (Crown Business/Random House), mapped how the internet was shifting power from brands to consumers—and planted the seeds that grew into this book.

Pete holds an MBA from **Harvard Business School** and a bachelor's degree from the **University of California, Santa Cruz**—where, among other things, he co-created the logo for the school's iconic mascot, the Banana Slug. He lives in Cincinnati, Ohio.

# Index

## B

## C

## D